Presented
to the library
by
John
Simon

Selected Poems

Selected Poems

by ENNIS REES

with 9 monoprints by Robert L. Nance

UNIVERSITY OF SOUTH CAROLINA PRESS
Columbia, South Carolina

The Odyssey of Homer, © Copyright, 1960, by Ennis Rees. The Iliad of Homer, © Copyright, 1963, by Ennis Rees. "The Death of Hector," from The Iliad of Homer, Books XVI, XVIII, and XXII, Copyright © 1963 by The University of the South. "Priam and Achilles," from The Iliad of Homer, Book XXIV, Copyright © 1963 University of Nebraska Press. Poems, Copyright © 1964 by The University of South Carolina Press. "Six Fables from Aesop," Copyright 1964 by Arion. "The Old Story," © 1965 Outposts Publications. "Primeval Apollo" and "Quite Certain," © Copyright 1965 by Red Clay Reader. Fables from Aesop, Copyright © 1964, 1966 by Ennis Rees.

FIRST EDITION

Published in Columbia, South Carolina, by the University of South Carolina Press, 1973

Library of Congress Cataloging in Publication Data

Rees, Ennis.
  Selected Poems.

PS3568.E4A6 1973   811'.5'4   73-7917
ISBN 0-87249-295-8
ISBN 0-87249-301-6 (pbk.)

To Marion

Note

In this selection, I have included most of the poems and fables from my book of 1964 and added a selection of poems written since, along with passages from my Homer. Of the new work, the long poem "Daze" was written in 1965, the sequence "Snakes and Butterflies" more recently.

The poems "Quite Certain" and "Primeval Apollo" appeared originally in *The Red Clay Reader,* "The Old Story" in *Outposts,* certain of the fables in *Arion,* and selections from the *Iliad* in *Prairie Schooner* and *The Sewanee Review.* I would like to thank the editors for permission to reprint these poems here.

I would also like to thank Random House for permission to reprint the selections from the *Iliad* and the *Odyssey,* and the Oxford University Press for permission to reprint the selections from *Fables from Aesop.*

ENNIS REES
Columbia, S.C.

Contents

II New Poems

Daze

Snakes and Butterflies

III From Fables from Aesop

IV From the Iliad and the Odyssey of Homer

From The Iliad

From The Odyssey

A Note on the Author

1
From Poems (1964)

THE CYCLE OF GLEE

Watching the children
Today on the shore
Exulting in earth
And the gray sea's roar
I saw created
Through every hand
Fine houses and castles
And cities of sand
Which they destroyed
With even more glee
Than building had been
For them or for me
And what they left standing
The tide washed away
That they might rebuild
Again the next day.

PAPERBOY

Maybe ten years old
In a red leather cap
With earflaps awry

He stands in the cold
On the corner of Main Street
Crying the headlines:

"Nations split
On A-weapons issue."

HOW HE WOULD STAND THERE

When as a little boy he sat in school
And dreamt from early recess to crackle of lunch bags,
He always dreamt of killing a great bald eagle
Whose haunts were granite canyons, granite crags.

Triumphant, then, he would take the eagle home
And think how to conduct himself amid
What would be said, if he should ever come
With eagle home....Perhaps as David did.

He just stood there, still, sling unwound,
Eyes no longer on the severed head
Or bulk of bale stretched out along the ground,
And waited for them beside Goliath dead.

ESPECIALLY FOR COWBOYS

He came to town a stranger, quiet and strong,
Soon sought out the villains, brought them low.
The golden girl was his and his a song,
Full simple nasal numbers filled with woe.

One for whom no act had consequences
At all commensurate with what he'd done,
He rode through life not quite aware of fences,
A lad who fared poorly at first but always won.

Daily we followed his trail on our way to school.
He was all we admired and wished to ever be.
But we failed to catch up with him: we rode a mule.
Now he is all that we shall never be.

THE DISCOVERY

Small boy and smaller girl, they stood
Beneath the door of the pull-down stair
To the attic, where not yet disguised in tinsel

And foil their Christmas presents were stored,
Absolutely not to be seen by them
Till dawn of the birthday soon to be,

Forbidden knowledge indeed! But Mother
Was out still shopping and Maid was outside
Safely chatting with help from across the street.

Daring all, little sister reached up from a chair
And clutching the cord pulled the stairway down.
Then up the two climbed, still small enough

To mount side by side, and over the threshold
They peered, entranced with the bliss of not knowing,
Gay with anticipation. And there

In the gloom of the attic, in the light that spread
From the eaves, they saw the lovely new presents,
They stared in awe at the presents, and felt

However vaguely what they had to do,
And what would now be required of them,
And how little able they were to live

With such child-changing, almighty demands.

UNCAGED

In the middle of town on a warm fall day
Not long before the State Fair was to open,
A blue Chevrolet station wagon,
One man and the driver in the front seat

And in the rear, otherwise uncaged,
An African lion and a pacing leopard
Nuzzling the necks of the dusty pair
On the gnawed-up seat of the battered blue wagon

With the dim Texas plates—and a little girl
Nearby with her mother said, "Look, Mommy.
See the big dogs," and went back to staring
Into the store window, while across the street

The wagon pulled to the curb and stopped,
As also I, afoot and staring
For maybe a minute. The street was uncrowded
And apparently nobody else had noticed.

At last I said to the little girl,
"You don't see a lion like that every day."
"No, you sure don't," she murmured, still looking
Into the window there with her mother.

"It's a real lion," I said too quietly,
And then…"Oh gosh! It's a *real lion*!
Mommy, a leopard! Look over there—
A leopard, a lion, a LION! a LION!"

CIRCUS

First came the bobbing little brown and white dogs
To scamper and scud and explode the taut paper hoop,
To walk on hind legs, to dance their solemn stiff jigs
Before leaving the ring and circling the sawdust loop.

The elephants now with sad inelegant eyes
Glide in circles, waltz, and play London Bridge,
Sit on stools and are the fat and wise
Who lumbering leave with a grace both certain and large.

At top of tent the act of the evening starts
When a chalk-white glittering girl steps out on a wire.
She dips and dances there as hailing hearts
Leap loud, and sits in a chair rose-ringed with fire.

Say, little dogs, and say, ye fat intelligent
Pachyderms, is she not gracious there,
Enthroned on air, and is she not elegant,
And to dare with such blazing calm art, is she not rare!

VIGNETTES AND VOICES

1

Farewell

"This little bit of universe
  I absolutely will not share!"
Said the trapper with a curse
  As he was eaten by the bear.

2

Valentine

Dear Dickie Dogtooth here's my heart
  And pulse without a pause
Of course I'd like the same from you
  Your own dear Margie Catclaws.

3

Sport's Story

Not easy to scare,
  No lady fearer,
He died combing hair
  In the rear-view mirror.

4

In the Tent

Thank you for inviting, sir,
  Our girls to your revival,
But it's the coeds, not the codes,
  That will insure survival.

5

Cloud Break

Momentary
  Relief of pain:
Iridescent
  Criss-cross rain.

6

The Difference

"The cosmic and the comic,
  How far apart, how far?"
To be quite economic,
  A wagon and a star.

7

Compensation

Gnarled nose, pig eyes, with other sad features,
  Who cares and what does it matter?
From back or front like all other creatures
  I cast a beautiful shadow.

11

8

At the Lecture

"Through time's assault and battery
  Two things always endure—
Poetry and pottery."
  Mister, are you sure?

9

Interval

A moment minus
  Push or pull
Is a moment of love
  Illimitable.

10

Hail!

Hail to cities of future men!
  Gone Rome and Samarkand,
When all the land is sea again
  And all the sea is land.

DRYADS

Tree for me is spangled in the spring
At sunrise—trunk and branches leap
With luminous leaves like life of bareback rider,
Slender circus girl, at whom we stare
Astonished at grace incarnate blossoming
In spangles sparsely clad in smoky tent.

Tree for me is sequined in the fall
At sunset—trunk and branches spill
Plum-bright leaves, consumptive-maiden-like,
Who in a smoky atmosphere gives fragile
Sense of summer fruit to us appalled
At sinking sap so plum-bright sequined red.

REMINDER

Here sits one with powdered jowls,
Angry, large, and vicious.
Another tans among the towels,
Melting, pert, delicious.

But out in all those other worlds
That float and roll like ours,
What ogres roam, what dainty girls
Stretch among the flowers?

No other has our wide verandas,
Or busy, jowly ladies,
Our warm and wondering Mirandas,
Betty Jeans and Sadies.

TO LITTLE DIANNE, ON ICE

Embracing all the open rink
  The snow is blue
As moonlight shines down on the pink
  And white of you.

You smile at us, just once, how nice,
  Then to your solo,
Your quick silver cutting the rose-lit ice.
  How cold the warm glow!

I see you ten years from now, Dianne,
  The snow all melted,
And you still in white on the arm of some man,
  Departing rice-pelted.

You leave them all there, and among the bright misses
  A bouquet caught.
Your way through their lives has been light as your kisses,
  No juggernaut.

But this time no solo, Dianne: a duet,
  With the ice orchid-thin.
Still you, you're the gay and the gracious one yet—
  Here's to you, then.

SMALL CHANGE

Something said I knew her
  But I didn't.
So when the waiter went
  To change the dollar
I'd given him in payment
  For the coffee,
I followed down the counter
  To behind
The corduroy skirt
  She wore that morning.

Then something made me muff
  The handed change
And spill about her head
  Bright dimes and pennies,
Through which she smiled
  And looking up said, "Hi."
And I, "I didn't know you—
  It's your hair.
You've changed the way you wear it."
  "Oh," said she,
"I have for now.
  You've always seen it up."

And it was down,
  Blonde and flipped and shining.
And then I knew
  What made me drop the change.

JOY RIDE

Her head sways gracefully
Back and aside
As the sports car turns
The corner,

She and her date
Off on a ride,
Mary
And Little Jack Horner.

And our eyes meet
As the car blurs by,
Throbs into gear
And is gone—

A burst of light
Blonde hair on the sky
And eyes
As green as the lawn.

COPPER AND BLUE

We lived down by and across the railroad tracks
In a shack that leaked and the wind blew through
And she every day would come home at night
From her work in the city. Her hair was copper

And she in love with all shades of blue.
And every day I would go up and down
In the streets that nobody knew, looking for nothing,
Though once I saw an old friend who waved

From a car that was as it seemed unable to move
Beneath a broken traffic light. But he was gone
Before I could get there, and I as usual glad
Every day to go home at night to the shack that leaked

And the wind blew through. She was glad too
And would shake her copper hair and change her lovely
Blue dress. Of course it all came to nothing at last.
It was a strange existence, and at times we weren't very
    happy.

MOMENT OF DARKNESS

The waitress has spilled coffee on her apron
And sandalled feet are somewhat scarred and torn,
But as she bends to wipe the lacquered table
Her flesh is born from frankincense again,
With help of low blue lights and balmy summer.

The nurse's figure, uniformed in white,
Undulates sea-mystery as she walks,
For much of her is dark though opulent
And more alive than hawks or hopelessness
With challenge for some champion to arise.

The moment of the body is our moment
Of the mind, starchy, fragrant, and right,
Ropy and terrible, as Grendel's dam
Makes off into the night with Aeschere
And Grendel's own lost bloody battered arm.

THE PARTING

She turned, he turned
They clutched each other

He turned, she turned
They left each other

And walked insensibly through
An insufferable August day

On which the dogs and birds
Were going quietly about

Their unequivocal business.

DEFIANCE

Oh my Lord the pride of her,
The wry smile from inside of her,
The perfumed and powdered hide of her,
And that go-to-hell yellow dress!

And then my Lord the stride of her!
Every part was surely tried of her,
Though women and men had lied of her
With that blue rose in her hair.

But jeers and cheers went wide of her.
All that was implied of her
Simply made a bride of her!
With that go-to-hell yellow dress
And that blue rose in her hair.

THE BETTER WAY

The tree I saw this morning
Blown over and half uprooted
Could not be saved. Last year
They painfully propped and replanted
A storm-plowed one very like it,
Tended and watered it well
Only to have it die
By degrees and rot. So before
Night came this one was sawed
And chopped and split, golden
From heart to bark, divinely
Good for various things
And to keep a house warm all winter.

TABLEAU

Her hair drawn back
   In a bun,
Her trunk curving up
   From the earth
Like a lissome young
   Coconut palm,
She stands
   In mute adoring
Of Tweedles
   Below in the pram,
While around them
   Summer is dying
And twilight
   Already begun.

THE NATURAL SOLUTION

In the middle of
  Their journey
They found themselves
  In the woods,
The dark, unfriendly
  Woods.

So they built a cabin
  There
And started to raise
  A family,
Which in a decade
  Numbered ten.

How can one be
  Afraid
In the dark, unfriendly
  Woods
When the woods are full of
  Children?

"BALLROOM"

They brought the girls in buggies and on foot
To dance at Mrs. Sloan's, where she instructs.
From fall to spring they brought them twice a month
In dazzling party shoes and party frocks.

And Mrs. Sloan would greet them on the threshold
And introduce them to the little boys.
Then toy couples whirled upon the dance-floor
Delightfully increasing in their poise.

Then they came in cars, in Model-T's,
In Buicks, Dodges, Cadillacs, Corvairs.
And some I brought myself, five at a time,
Sandra, Beth, Dianne, Celeste, and Claire.

They talked about the boys going home
And laid their plots in charity and charm.
They learned to flirt and flee at Mrs. Sloan's
And give a graceful form to gaiety.

They waltzed at Mrs. Sloan's for fifty winters
And lingered on her lawn in first romance.
So homage to this lady, grand and gracious,
Who taught three generations how to dance.

A FEW LAST WORDS FROM THE OLD DISPENSATION

Just as the foe was closing in,
His bowstring broke—what then?
"Cut several strands of your long black hair,"
He said to his wife behind him there,
"And twist me a string to use on my bow."
And she, looking out on the charging foe,
Said, "Tell me now, as I am your wife,
Does it mean much to you?" "It means my life,"
The warrior said. "Twist the strands well."
"Ah," she answered, "now I can tell
That you have forgot that vicious slap
You gave me one day just after your nap.
No bowstring you'll get from me, I fear."
"No what?" said he. "No bowstring, dear."
"Well," he replied, with a thin white smile,
"None of us lives but a little while
And each must win fame in a way of his own.
Let this be yours and yours alone
So long as there's breath for what never ceases."
And the foe broke in and hacked them to pieces.

In a white lace dress with a spray of red roses
Priscilla was Queen of the May.
The bearing so regal that rarely she loses
Stood her in good stead today.

When, though, her Court had all been assembled,
Miss Butterflies entered the aisle.
No girl in the world who wouldn't have trembled
As Priscilla did for a while.

But then she regained her royal composure
And tilted her head in the air
Quite like the brave Psyche tasting ambrosia.
Who can with Priscilla compare?

Enthroned at last in ephemeral splendor
With scarcely a May Day to shine,
Priscilla was Queen with queens to attend her.
Farewell, O daughter of mine.

THE UNACCEPTABLE

Her morning gift
Lies at the door again,
The white cat's kill
Of lizard and of bird.
Duly she brings all back
To mortgaged men,
Who look with nausea
And spew one ugsome word.

At least once a year
She scratches the front screen door
And runs through my legs
With a whole squirrel in her jaws,
Bringing raw death in the house,
And bloody spoor,
And everywhere panic
Till out the back door go her paws.

Then under low holly she lies,
Munching her kill
In an unknown feline state,
As if to grieve,
Having proudly brought home
What none of us had the will
Or courage, or grace,
Or happiness to receive.

COMMENTARY

We don't look up
At the famous general
Whose mineral statue
Stands in the park
Oxidizing and green

Nor does the pigeon
Perched on his head
Dishonoring the dead
With his foul mark
And scandalizing the scene.

LINES FOR AN ACTRESS

She wasn't really
What most people thought her to be,
For that was a lie
Made up by fat profiteers,

Bringing her fame
That quickly brought her to see
How little a girl she was,
How great were her fears.

But the callous brute myth
Mushroomed and was pernicious,
Choking the real little girl
Searching for Daddy,

And all of us used her,
Dumb lechers grinning and vicious,
Till no breath at all was left
In her talented body.

A CAT WHERE ROSES GREW

Alley cat in a landscape
Of sedge. Below him a ditch,
Behind him a hedge. His body
A hump, his head a wedge.

There are no other cats around.

This one is watching something,
One supposes,
Or waiting for something,
One isn't sure:
But sitting there
Where roses grew last summer,
This cat in a landscape of sedge,
Behind him a hedge, his head a wedge,
Is to one passing in a car
A sight more rare,
If less fair,
Than roses are by far.

His family once played the Coliseum.

PERCHERS AND CHIRPERS

The sun was down at the end of the cracked old street
Where I'd seen it so when the failing branches froze.
In winter, in summer we have the red concrete
At sunset and the windows aflame with ruby and rose.

In summer dusk I watched them going to roost,
Those downy dark birds, in a tree where they perched and chirped
At a time when the street was still and the little breeze lost
In the leaves, which the twilight twittering wholly usurped.

As there on the sheltering, shadowy branches they perched,
And changed and chattered and chirped those winged words,
I by the talking tree stood fast and searched
Till I saw them asleep in the deep quiet, the deep peace of birds.

ELEGY FOR FALLING OBJECTS

Murderous
Matrons
Perambulate
On the pier.

The carousel
Horses lie
On their sides,
Dark holes
In their
Painted bellies.

Ralegh's head
Falls thud
On the scaffold,
And another
Summer is gone.

ASIA

MARCH 1959

when the Chinese invaded Tibet
and the Dalai Lama fled

Now the young high priest of Tibet's invisible ocean,
Grand Lama of the spirit, meek descendant
Of a migrant monkey and cave-cavorting banshee,
Reared on Writ and reverence and cheap

Brick tea from China, this in exchange for wool
And musk and gold and enriched with dung of the Yak,
Drifts and bobs on horseback through his unfactoried
Land, past prayer wheels and lamaseries,

Up the old caravan road southward and seaward,
Spiraling down the whole world's highest mountains,
World with which his country has little to do,
Threading the passes, floating over the rises

And across the windy plateaus, leaving a land
So high and cold that many make no attempt
To heat their hovels, in slow procession winding
Nightly nearer the heart of India,

Fleeing from hordes of idolatrous, violent converts
To sufficient bread, no riddles, and ruthless, dire
Expansion: his faith Reality, invisible lotus,
Fathomless rose, to which he knows all exiles

Must return through journeys of confusion,
Fire, and famine, escaping, if they do,
The illusory abyss of desperate self,
Dark haunt of the Abominable Snowman.

ACKNOWLEDGMENT

Oh how sweetly Lily Prim
Gave her life among us,
Serving, as she put it, Him
Who would not ever wrong us.

Seeing the sick and teaching school
Was the medium she worked in,
Angel to the thug and fool
And the shadow world they lurked in.

Memories of her on one afternoon
Like another View of Toledo
Return with the strains of an old hymn tune
And the hope that was her credo.

GOOD TIMES

In the world's
Invisible blood
We move,
Corpuscular,

Most happy when
St. Paul
Can freely travel
Roman roads,

Or Baedeker says,
As a few generations ago:
"Passports
May be dispensed with."

TO A BUG IN A WATERBOWL

One squirt
From the faucet
For you
Would have meant
The journey down
But haply
You were spared
To explore
Perpendicular porcelain,
Seemingly lost amid
A sunken
Antarctic waste,
A scarcely discernible
Mite
Moving off
In all directions,
But unexpectedly soon
Going back
To the hole
In the bottom
To await
With perfect acceptance
In the place
Of certain vortex
Your Charybdis
And sudden Niagara.

HOW LOVELY WITH CLAWS

I witness
That
Was a gorgeous
Cat
Black orange and
White
In a circle of
Light
On the asphalt
Road
Disemboweling a
Toad.

MID-WINTER

The morning sun
Glints diamond glare
From automobile
To automobile.

From telephone pole
To telephone pole
The swagged wires sway
In the gray afternoon.

The lights on later
Shaded shine
From house to house
In frozen streets.

COLD MORNING

Dead dog propped up
At a sixty degree
Like a trotting fox
Against a high curb
In front of St. Joseph's
Episcopal Church,
His stick legs broken
Before and behind,
His tongue frozen out
In a white grisly grin,
While sparkling green grass
And creamy white clouds
Dry and drift
Beneath the brave sun
On this the fairest
Of summer days,
On this the coldest
Of mornings for him.

LEGEND

On a street of the little town
When I first saw him alive
With the bushy iron-gray hair
And baggy old turtle-neck sweater
He loomed much larger than life
(For a birthday surprise they hired
The Budapest String Quartet
To play his favorite selections—
"At breakfast I'd like them to play,"
He said. "All day I'll be working")
And glowed with an aura of sweetness
And light, of healing and goodness
And grace: a quite incredible
Gray apparition, eating
An ice-cream cone, with nothing
(He sailed his boat on the lake,
A drop in the ocean of time,
Picked pebbles up on the shore
As the good Sir Isaac before him
And supported liberal occasions)
At all to do with the breaking
Of glass, the crashing of timber,
The evaporation of steel,
The disappearance of people
And worlds in rubble and ruin.

CELEBRATION OF SNOW

The breathless branches of trees are full of cold
That lasts for many days beneath the sun,
Limbs beneath the moon becoming blue.
The countryside is comfortably clad

In mystery as white as spring is green,
As keen as spring is keen. Past pale blue buildings
The crazy snow still falls and upward floats,
Floats and falls, and we watch it through ice-blue windows

From chairs that give on a cornerless crystalline world.
Already the snow is deep, but subtle and soft
As Helen's hair, white as the surplice worn
At joyful but now ill-attended ceremonies.

Somehow it reminds us—perhaps it's the great transformation
Over which we have little control—of the ominous howling
Of dogs we everyday hear as on our way home
We pass the experimental laboratory.

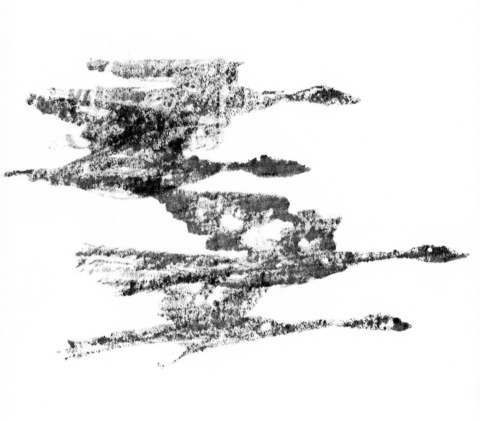

THE GRAY GEESE

A not very willing but very old man went with us
To see the gray geese, the countless gray geese that stop
Every year at this one particular pond, as they
Fly south for the winter. But once he got there I thought

We would never get him to leave. He stood mid the hooting
And honking and waddling and stretching of wings in a spell
Of some kind, till all of a sudden somebody quite close
Fired a gun and all of the geese took off as one bird

In a booming gray cloud that enveloped us all, and soon
They were gone. "I guess we can go now," said the very old man,
"And come back next year, perhaps, when the gray geese are here."
It was certainly something to see and look forward to

And it's true they come every year without fail in great numbers.

A FEW COLD DAYS

1

A dark day,
   The foggy road
And the vertical rain.

2

The hum of the tires
   Spattering drops,
The headlights white through the drizzle.

3

The dog barks
   From his place by the fire.
Startled, I go on reading.

4

The frozen lake,
   Crossed and criss-crossed
By skaters at sunset.

5

Just over the pines at dusk,
   The light underside of a hawk
Reflecting the sun.

6

The empty streets,
   The streetlights burning,
A newspaper blown in the gutter.

7

To look at the moon
    I pull the curtain aside,
My shadow big on the wall.

8

The door blows open.
    In walks a cat
Sparkling with snowflakes.

9

How deep the silence
    Between the clear sky
And the frostbitten earth!

10

How splendid the sunlit ivy
    Around an old oak tree
On this winter day!

II

New Poems

QUITE CERTAIN

On the moonlit beach
  Each to each
Their murmuring mixed
  With the scuff of the surf

And songs of The Platters
  Wafted their way
From the gown-swept open
  Deb-haunted dance floor

Where they'd left the others,
  She an athletic
Well-tanned well-read
  Not at all frenetic

Obtuse or loose
  All American Girl,
He happy there
  On the silken sand

And both of them clear,
  Though their eyes were shut,
As to where they were
  And for what.

THE HYPOCHONDRIAC

His insecurity was much greater than yours,
My friend, unless you too are dependent on chores
And bores and are constantly in need of a place
To localize an Angst. All this the face

Of this man faintly showed, and when he laughed
The sound came straining out as if painfully coughed
Through a grill of fear, its function to defend.
At fifty he decided he would spend

(Though otherwise more thrifty no one could be,
Since "Nothing in this world," he said, "is free."
But a lonely man at fifty subtly deceives
The clutched clichés in which he says he believes.)

Whatever it took for doctors anywhere
To find the growth that he paid well to swear
He felt enlarging right behind his navel.
He made *them* swear that they were on the level

And so they were, but still they could not find
The itching carcinoma in his mind,
Though he of course was perfectly convinced.
"There's Something swelling there," said he, and winced.

And certainly there was, as you well know,
And it continued there to grow and grow
And with it a lifelong hatred of us all
Who differed from him in ways however small.

And that, brave reader, quite likely included you.
At eighty, struck down in the street, he died, it's true.
"That swelling Thing," the last they heard him say,
"It was about to get me anyway."

Pulling her chain of children
She weaves them through the car lot,
Then swings across the street

Where coiling and uncoiling on the walk
The little links unclasp
And run into the yard. There

She plays with them at hide-and-seek
And ring-around-the-roses, until
They tire and joining hands once more

Enclose her in a ring. Eerily
They sing, then fling themselves
Upon her, choking, scratching,

Trampling on her body, trampling
On her head, trampling, trampling,
Trampling till she wakes.

WEATHER REPORT

To be in a winter fog in the midst of things
Is bone to be in the breast of a great gray enfolding
Us bird, while above lie soft unfolding wings.
Around us the snow in dirty heaps lies melting,

The silhouette silent trees rise branchy and black
And people are shadows that pause, pass among puddles.
Here is a dimly daylit night of cloud rack
Rolling close, a colorless world that muddles

The mind but lives there in tropelessness for a time,
A numb dumb beautiful world unrelated to change
For a moment only, since winter's crystalline rime
Has long ago fallen on city and ranch and range,

And that we remember, though now in a feather of fog,
Till somehow the season changes and butterflies glow,
Glance, gleam in a light that fell on the rug
Last emerald year and follows new flowers now

Through furrows of again teeming tilth in winter fields,
And the trees are joking felicitous giants that burgeon
May for a month or more, for the fog yields,
And people are vivid and gay as the searing surgeon

Mind escapes the great gray breast and bone
Of the brooding us bird, now in a miracle of makers,
The one become many and still remaining one,
We in winter walking mid soarers and singers.

PRIMEVAL APOLLO

Tired of chewing
  On the snake
He thought of something
  He could make

And bending the stick
  He had in his hand
He strung it taut
  With a twisted strand

Then plucked away
  With a gleeful grin
On the only lyre
  That had ever been

Till another savage
  Said, "Come on, boys,
Let's make him stop
  That plucking noise!"

Whereat the gleeman
  Showed his ire
By putting a stick
  To the string of his lyre

Thus making what later
  He would know
As the god-given first
  Almighty bow

And pulling it back
  That bard troglodytic
Enlightened the heart
  Of the first angry critic.

PARAPLEGIASTES

The whole thing happened so fast.
The left-side blinker was broken
And I was wandering, oblivious
Of the moment, musing of
A scarfed and muffled afternoon
Where players fade forever for a pass,
Of how I never knew her maiden name,

Of Plato, Jesus, and then a young Nazi
Bulldozing bodies, of bodies, dark bodies
So obscured by Saturday night that
Cars run over them until it's light,
Of a box, a cage, productive of rage,
Of one bellyache and one barked shin,
Of oh what a mess this world is in

And after the crash nobody came
For two hours, and then it was over,
And now it is over, and now
A moment of fatigue when flesh itself
Seems strange beyond belief,
The whole thing like nothing so much
As backing over the baby.

And now, having come so close to the end,
It makes me sick, as if
I didn't deserve to live,
Being that unwary, and life's become
Too much of a gift, striking me
Harshly, harshly, as I bend to tie
A shoelace in the sun.

For watching the dying trees
That weep their snow in this
December thaw, I know the snows
Must go, as every year,
And where are they? Gone with all
The rivulets of April, gone
With the roiling rivers of grievous May.

And now, I still don't live in the present
As I sit here watching the traffic.
But ah, the world, my world!
It's oystershell toward dawn
And apricot toward night, and in between,
The sun and other stars, they fade
From surgical red to clinical white.

ILLUMINATION

Like the curious ape in the fable
I got caught by a half-split log
I too from inattention
Withdrawing the blade while my fingers
Were down in the new-sprung cleft

One way to be reminded
How wholly a part of things
We are, nature latching on
To us, painlessly, painfully, inside
And outside, which may help explain
The numbly silent scene
That kept on flashing before me
As I frantically parted the log
Once again with the blade of the ax

A scene in the snow-filled mountains
Of a giant passenger jet
Illuminating the flakes
As it glided in to crash
At night on the frozen peaks
Its wings clipped one at a time
As it hurtled past crag after crag
To explode at last in the snow
One awful flower of flame.

THE OLD STORY

"With birth," he said,
"The situation
Changes, and soon

I was a man
Twisting across a chasm
Hand over hand

Along an endless wire
Till numb
With weariness and terror

I dropped.
The water below was bracing,
Green islands everywhere."

Daze

PART ONE

1

Again the time is come
For a bard of dross and dreaming to begin
And build the lofty rhyme.
Lofty, yes, or low,
Depending on the sense contained therein,
But lyre at work or banjo
This epos sings a life in a kind of diary
Of the sad and glad and bad and just plain sorry.

2

We'll need some names of course,
One for Mother and one for Father too.
Well, they're a bit flat for verse
And not at all refined,
But Fred and Fay, alas, will have to do.
These days we're in a bind
About such folks, since they, like us, are far
From being half-way sure just what they are.

Something we're bound to be
And so far as feeling goes we've made a myth
That says the will is free.
Logic, here, is out
And Fred and Fay feel freer with a fifth
Inside of them and shouting
That life's a process and therefore so are we
And the best thing for a process is feeling free!

Some record of the process,
Of how it looks and sounds, may help us prize it,
Of how it tastes and smells
And acts and feels and talks.
All this and more may help to humanize it
And here no true bard balks
But renders and, like any scholar, delves
That we may better learn to know ourselves.

That sober declaration
Is to help uneasy readers to relax.
For in every nervous nation
There're many who refuse
To read at all, except for useful facts.
With those how can you lose?
But really, reader, before this stanza's done,
I must confess I wrote it all in fun.

4

As feeling summons sound
From the moiling dark of correspondences
Likenesses abound
As word calls out to word
Discovering as well unlikenesses,
All this our real reward:
The music and the metaphor of rhyme
Which making I affirm and reaffirm.

If you don't like a verse
"Turne over the leef and chese another tale,"
   As a predecessor terse
   Advises (yes, but where?)
And you may hit a line more to your liking, scholar,
   A verse both full and fair
That welled its way from somewhat greater depths
And so will glow more brightly on your lips.

PART TWO

1

One element of fate
That Fred and Fay had always had in common
    Was an unfortunate
    Parental situation
In which on either side both Daddy and Momma
    Had miserably alternated
Between indulging the children and screaming at them.
It's a wonder that the children didn't hate them.

2

At twenty-one Fay thought
She'd best enroll in some good graduate school,
    She having already bought,
    As imagination can,
The rugs and kitchen stove and ornate bowl
    Before she met the man
Who numbly purchased all of that and more
And paid by working nights in a cut-rate store.

And at first they disagreed
Though raised in two quite similar hometowns,
    Uncertain in their creed,
    "Interested in art,"
And neither one quite up to settling down.
    Together but apart
They rehearsed old hometown roles of maudlin sorrow,
With "Oh, farewell to Sodom," but "Hail, Gomorrah!"

3

When reading Mother Goose
They taught the baby, Daze, a rhyme or two
　　Which helped to make a truce
　　Whenever she performed
For friends with "One, two, buckle your shoe"
　　And oh how feelings warmed
And oh what laughing pride the parents felt
When once it came "One, two, buckle your—seat-belt."

　　Blindly feuding one day
When the two-year-old was with them in the car,
　　"You never like my way!"
　　Kept ringing back and forth
Till even the baby said it as from afar.
　　"I know what you are worth!"
Came next, and then "You know what I can't stand!"
And then in the car-door slammed was baby's hand.

4

　　A great live oak, pre-Columbian
In mossy years, beneath whose awesome boughs
　　Passed many an Indian
　　Where later muslined girls
Strolled with their beaux and sat exchanging vows—
　　And there against its bole
One April day Fay said to Fred, "You jerk!
All you think of is your stupid work!"

Perhaps her most telling remark,
A banality like the rest but entre nous
Made when the room was dark
And she resuming her gown,
Was "Pooh! You're just too goddam stupid to be true!"
At which he probably frowned.
She never knew, but such banalities
Had come to be their chief realities.

5

The buff of the breeze on her face,
The skitter of leaves, the chitter, the chatter of birds,
The pounce and bounce of the squirrel,
Its crouch in the crotch of the elm,
The breath of the pondy water, glisten of mud,
The feathery air about her,
Daze swished her feet in the amber, attracting the bream,
Daze wriggled her toes in the ooze, rubbed her back on a limb.

6

Then came the sullen years,
When every other month they did not speak,
Endurance tests and tears
Well mixed with intimacies
And periods when the proud were suddenly meek
And weak: ill, that is.
For "the surly bird gets the germ"—so say the wise,
And slowly torment taught them compromise.

Thus nature pulled two ways
Within herself and hardly seemed to know
    In which direction lay
    The appointed goal.
But something worked to fuse them, and although
    They scarcely were one soul,
At least they'd overcome the painful odds
Of processing two egos and their gods.

7

For a while they were half-aware
That what they did together was a game
    And they didn't really care
    When some surprising ploy
Showed their vows were pretense all the same.
    In fact it gave them joy.
But now they'd played so long they had forgot
It was a game. No need to pretend it was not.

After a decade or so
They seldom disagreed, at least in words,
    Which they had come to know
    In senses that were unique
And only to outsiders quite absurd.
    At least three times a week
They reconfirmed their world of flesh and bone
In those sweet terms that now were all their own.

In twenty dwindling years
Their world of words had thickened and drawn in
        Enough to cause some fears
        Even in their children,
Who all unconsciously had mostly been
        A chorus of little women
And little men reverberating in
The echo chamber that was home to them.

                        8

        "Oh him—he's such a dope,"
Or her, no matter, they usually agreed
        On parlor guest or Pope
        With ice-eyed valuing
That seldom went beyond "Oh what a creep!"
        A kind of hardening
With counters of rejection they'd exchange
Till nothing in the world was new or strange.

        It was a universe
Conveniently built with wall of glass,
        An invisible kind of curse,
        For soon they found that though
They could see outside, outside they could not pass,
        And they were frightened so
They started to speak quite well of those inside,
But those without they just could not abide.

Inside apparently
They felt a mountain safer than some folk
    Who suffer from diseases
    A sea less serious.
For the one they had contracted was no joke.
    In truth it was a kind
Of mental dystrophy, an arteriosclerosis
Of the mind, and with it an increasing deep narcosis.

PART THREE

1

But what demands our praise
Of all that Fred and Fay produced and reared?
    It was their daughter Daze,
    Or Daisy Eloise,
And she day's eye indeed, by envy feared,
    Though loving her was easy
And her name quite right, since a daze is what most men,
After one look at her, lost themselves in.

    Daze wasn't perfect of course.
What's that? Nor did she care to be,
    She not above using force
    Of fierce and sundry kinds,
But especially deception, subtlety,
    To change unwilling minds.
As for perfection, though, she'll have to do
Till nature combines the cat and cockatoo.

2

    But what redeemed her?
Some love from out the aeons of her making
    Appearing in her life.
    For Nothing's first, she thought,
Though surely it's as if the sea were first,
    A sphere encircling all
In which reflected is the changing sky,
Another sphere, the cream and golden clouds,

The thunderheads, tornadoes
And all that hisses hail into the sea,
The miles of mist and snow
And rain renewing all
With water and with life that way beginning.
What salt grotesquerie
In those first awful gasping muddy days!
What floundering of flippers and of fins

As surf gave way to sand!
What deaths and resurrections on those shores!
"The Father," murmured Daze,
"Reflected in the Mother,
The Father pours his rain into her sea
Absorbing all
And from her sea on earth at last appearing
Their slimy offspring dance upon the sand."

3

Queen Daze, of sun and fun,
No season's end without her loud election
To Miss Oh Gorgeous! To run
Was sure to win, and deftly,
Since no one walked a ramp with more perfection
Or charmed a judge more swiftly.
She smiled, she sang—oh more, far more than cute
Was lovely Daze, in evening gown or swim suit.

But Daze made the same mistake
In the world of beauty queens and corporate machines
That as a child she'd made
In assuming her parents knew
What they were doing, that someone had hold of the reins.
It wasn't true.
There was no bit or bridle on the horse
And its rider, Pumpkin Head, was at a loss.

4

She strummed the strings, she sang,
No voice than hers more moving, low or high,
And traveled with a gang
Of bluejeaned balladeers,
All twangling bards and scops of liberty.
Her gleemen chanticleers,
They read to her from Homer and Li Po
And she'd say, "Now hear this, from sweetie-pie Thoreau."

Her favorite was little Leroy,
Who played the bass and sang with gospel vim,
A Negro boy
With rhythm (they said) in his genes.
Daze called him Bunny and sang duets with him
From Boston to New Orleans.
Leroy sang and talked when he wasn't eating
Or "doing his job"—which he said was mostly reading.

"Those rabid sharks," said he,
"That swam up from the depths of Naziism
    Have access in the dark
    To all the oceans
Including our own, and they're drawn by the blood of schism."
    "Why Leroy, what funny notions!"
"Fun-n-nee!" said Daze. "Oh jumping jism, Bess,
Change! or children will lie in the streets—all colorless!"

                              5

    An old sedan,
Dull red and white, dark blood-colored mud on the wheels,
    The driver a red-faced man
    Undergoing a chewing-out
From the work-worn scraggly woman who got his meals,
    The back seat filled with a rout
Of half-bare streaky children. "If that's what we're
    up against,"
Said Bess, "we're dead." "And that's not all," Daze said.

                              6

    "Oh we work hard, you know,
On the county histories and General Lee
    And thank the Lord our Nigras
    Are all well satisfied.
They couldn't be more happy or—well, free,"
    She sighed.
"Oh shoot," said Daze. "These oleander ladies
Will help us even less than did their daddies."

7

The twist, the frug, the jerk,
Daze danced on beaches, in discotheques-a-go-go,
While the fountains in the park
Joined in the wild Watusi
And the summer stars fell dancing through the dark.
"Have you ever noticed," said Lucy,
"How when Daze dances, everything seems to dance?"
"But everything does," said Leroy. "Will you, perchance?"

8

The sun, thought Daze, comes
Bringing us Asia daily, flooding each home
And hamlet with luminously
Empty Eastern air,
The light that broke upon the open road
Where we relaxed, alert
Begin and end in light that shows all dancing
Of itself and reconfirms our faith primordial.

The future lies below
Unknown as central earth from whence it surges.
The pull of love
The pull of gravity
It is one pull and draws us to the center,
Vertical as always,
A fountain playing brightly in the glade
Beneath the hovering past, it too unknown,

A playing in the present,
A thrust forever upward toward the zenith,
A living Now
In which the past is present
Falling in the fountain, sprinkling round,
In which all lore becomes
Elixir that infuses love and learning,
The ancient esoteric sweet arcane.

9

Daze wept for Himey Saul
Who died hysterically with blood all sticky
Trying to creep or call.
She wept and wept,
Recalling summer days she'd spent with Himey
And laughing nights
With him before he left. She wept for Jim,
Her other soldier gone. She wept—for both of them.

"War's vile," she sobbed,
"Vile murder, vile—vile murder, murder, murder!"
"But there're reasons for war," said the doctor.
"None good enough," she cried.
"Not nearly! Such killing is filthy murder—murder
      unjustified
By reasons, no matter what—all filthy vile!
Not worth the life of one small yellow child!"

10

Then one night after dinner
She left the house and walked—for nineteen miles,
    One mile for each of her years
    (Fred frantic, Fay in tears)
Then called, from a highway phone at 2 a.m., the doctor,
    Who came and took her home.
"Are you ready now," he asked, "to start again?
I think we've both about had it." Said Daze, "Amen."

At school she met a fellow
Whose dearest doctrine was original sin.
    Calvin he fancied ("Calvin who?"
    She queried) and Schopenhauer
Plus other ruinous men. "All poisoners—ooh!"
    Said Daze, "the dour sour!"
And as for the doctrine, she said she would rather doubt it,
That though it was sinful, there was nothing original about it.

    Another kept repeating
Some mumble-jumble about "the inner man."
    "But," said Daze, "take eating,
    Or breathing, if you'd rather."
Another nursed "objective," another hugged "plan."
    "Oh frou-frou!" she fumed. "Oh bother!
We're part of it all, you know, or to put it terser,
No outside without an inside, and vice versa."

"In a universe," said one,
"That we can't conceive nor even describe at all well
    In terms of multidimensional
    Mathematics, elation
For us is what we perceive as real and think and feel
    In a lifetime's observation
Of mystery infolding, unfolding more and more."
"Hear, hear," Daze whispered. "Sweetie, this is an encore!"

12

"You are," said Daze to date,
"A creep to end all creeps, an arrested caterpillar
    Slug-slimy crawly wormy
    Copperheaded creep!"
In the glare of her eyes the creep saw Daze the killer
    And wriggled to leap
And run from house to car, preserving life,
As from her hand Daze dropped the carving knife.

13

I fear that Daze annoyed
A host of people, she being—well hardly outspoken,
    But blithely she destroyed
    Her share of idols. A word,
A phrase or two, a look, and they were broken
    And squalidly absurd.
With dogmatists she'd wait until they ceased.
Then "Nothing's final," she'd say. "No word at least."

The female barren bluffs,
The brittle males, were critical and chill
Whenever their beliefs
Were shattered and eroded
By Daze at home or Daze at a posh motel.
The clam, the cluster, she goaded,
But mostly it was coldness she abhorred.
"I will," she said, "be thoroughly explored."

14

"One exploding fact,"
Said Daze, "obliterates philosophy—
The fact that we are here,
Unspeakably astounding,
Obliterates all thin theosophy."
"Ye gods and grace abounding,
Daze, what turns you on?" "Ye gods, my dear,
And the sun, the moon, the stars—but mostly we, here!"

PART FOUR

1

As Daze came down the aisle
On the arm of Fred her father she recalled
An old professor's question:
"Was Blake mad?"
At which she smiled, thus radiant to all.
"Mad people sing,"
She thought, and knew him mad, divinely so,
And winked at vapid virgins in a row.

Not so their marriage began,
But in that haze of June when they were children
Digging the brookside, and Dan,
Grasping what seemed a crook
Of rusty pipe, enclosed a moccasin
That slid off through his hand
Into the stream, and Daze sat with him there
To shiver with him, to share primeval fear.

2

Rain in a sea-side town,
Their honeymoon, a resort where they'd meant to splurge,
Rain drizzling all around
On furrowed bay and field
As land and sea and sky all seemed to merge
Till all things were concealed
In the grayest rain, the softest rain there is,
Sweet solvent of their tense polarities.

Call me shining, sweet,
Call me drifting amber, call me crescent,
Call me pigeon's neck,
Call me opalescent,
Call me shining, sweet, and iridescent,
    And I will call you ocean,
Earth, and dawn, I'll call you rain and cry,
And then I'll call you snake and butterfly.

3

Daze to her obstetrician,
He checking, she chatting, she an old friend of his,
    "You heard him—what an ambition
    For a polititian! Besides,
He's a jug of (oh! don't squeeze) of phoney fizz,
    Mostly bromides."
"Uh huh, I (hold it, Daze) could've told you that,
Known the bastard forever—Daze, you're getting too fat."

And naked in front of her glass,
As slowly filled her veined, voluptuous vessel,
    "Oh Coke-bottle me, alas,
    Now more like an amphora urn,
Curves from potters primeval, evokers of whistles,
    All for the cruel unborn,
Leading me, leading me, on to the sacrifice,
Shearing me, tearing me—genes, you're not very nice!"

So Daze was the mother of twins,
But dreamed at night her husband was a horse,
The horse she'd ridden
Daily when she was thirteen.
She'd loved his rippling bronze and gentle force
And felt herself a queen
As on him she rode through the fields of afternoon
And, dreaming, galloped him hard across the moon.

But now regality wilted
Beneath routine of dust and baby care
And matrons stultified.
Oh still Daze loved to ride—
In her new Jaguar now through the dieseled air
Past the Jesus Is Coming Soon signs
And the heron-stiff figures of farmers, she blithely gunning,
But she missed the pomp and being out of the running.

Jesus Is Coming Soon,
The sign slipped by. "Me too," she thought, and grinned.
For in her opinion
Blasphemy was invented
By clergymen who say Christ never sinned.
Daze never repented
For feeling good and bad God everywhere
And to Daze even goddam was a low form of prayer.

She dreamed by night, by day
And once that she was a sow as big as a city
Who lay with the Prince in a sty
As muddy big rich as the world,
The prince exploring his prize so fat and pretty
From dugs to mahogany hams
While those outside the pen cried shame all night
Till she awoke and found herself Snow White.

The warm life in shirt sleeves
In dusty suburbs selling real estate,
Burking builders,
Bilking buyers,
Was husband Dan's unchosen, choking fate.
"Oh dirt!" he cried, "I'm tired
Of what's the deal and angle? what's the take?
Of all these whores and hucksters on the make."

They made a home together,
Hearth, halls, and garden with pansied portico
All gorgeously transmuted
From mine and forest and quarry,
The home they said they would remember always,
Dreaming or awake,
A triumph over nature's viny chaos
Clarified from out her viscous blur.

But life half-good at first
Was sullen soon, then quibbles, squabbles, battles,
    As yellow years before
    And in another garden.
Handshadows for the children on the wall
    That used to mimic geese
Were howling wolves and hooded cobras now,
And life at home an all but ceaseless row.

8

    In dresses, skirts, and blouses,
All full of grace, all oh so full of Daze,
    In their own and others' houses,
    In toreadors tumescent,
Or shorts or slacks, her blithe and winsome ways
    Transformed the boors,
But sadly grew quiescent, though keener her claws,
As she made her dolorous errors, her fierce faux pas.

    She'd always let the moments
Take what shape they would, and so the hours,
    So the dancing years,
    All patterns choreographed
By who knows what infernal, supernal powers.
    But now she seldom laughed
As she grew tense and tenser, and what was worse,
She felt a nagging need to be perverse.

9

She awoke at 3 a.m.
To listen in terror for footsteps in the room,
　　Heard only sleeping him
　　And her own quick heart
Drumming the news of what she had become.
　　Thought she, "The tom-toms start,
And someday soon on planets Fu and Mars
We'll live in terror still among the stars."

　　Then Dan fled down a flight
Of ancient stairs and out into the garden
　　Where Daze sat in the moonlight
　　Submerged in the goldfish pool,
Only her lily head and neck like Nefertiti's
　　Above the teeming water.
"So," said Dan, "he seduced you—oh, the lout!"
"No," she said, "just plopped a goldfish inside out."

10

　　By the pain along her temples
Daze wanted a deeper communion than that of her parents.
　　"No deeper than Mother's dimples,"
　　She thought, recalling a snapshot
Of them in their serge and flowery holiday best
　　Frozen in front of a plot
In a formal garden, their death cold caught in the photo.
But she failed—Daze wanted an answer, her husband an echo.

At the argument's peak—bang!
They fought for the .22 pistol and fired it twice,
    Oh bang! hitting her once.
    How they shrank down the argument's slope!
And now how she missed being able to wash her own face,
    To which in the night she would grope,
Her wedding ring a throttling golden band,
Her diamond ring an ulcer on her hand.

11

    Go down, go down
Through murky ways beneath all towns and farms
    Descend with Daze, descend
    Where nothing can defend you,
Not wand of psychopomp nor the shaman's charms.
    Among the undead go
Where millions of bats deposit ghostly guano
And flitter from your mouth in endless swarms.

12

    They found Dan at his mother's
Curled up in the basement hugging an old rubber ball.
    "Why did you do it, son?"
    "The gun, it just went off."
"But why, why did you marry her at all?
    I knew she'd drive you wild.
Now what's to become of you, oh my poor child?"
"I guess I'll leave the twins with you awhile."

Daze heard the aimless tread
Of old ones scuffing the halls of their last home,
  Then saw them pale in bed
  As they stared at the common ceiling
And the glucose bottles that drip, soft metronomes.
  With a few, Daze shuffling, dealing,
The labs all busy, the surgeons brisk and strong,
The chaplain's office empty all day long.

  While Daze was thus restricted
She met a man recovering from a wound
  By wife and knife inflicted
  When he rejected echoes
And pressed so hard for answers she had found one.
  Hospitalized, with woes
In common, these two had time to play ping-pong and talk.
(Daze grinned at one young nurse inclined to gawk.)

  Visiting, Dan met
The knife-bewildered wife and was repelled.
  She told him all about it:
  "I was scared—I must have been."
In her blear eyes he saw his bleeding self.
  When Daze asked, "How're the twins?"
He said, "They miss you, Daze, and...so do I,"
Which made her cry, which finally made him cry.

14

    She dreamed she was lost in the woods,
Then locked in a building that people were bombing and burning.
    Escaping she found herself shut
    In the house of a family she knew,
Then suddenly back in the woods and running, running,
    Till out of breath she sat
In a ramshackle hut by the bed of a balmy crone
Who talked of her life in the sea, told all she had done.

PART FIVE

1

At home with Dan again
She found they'd changed in ways unlike their friends
And families. Dan
And she, not one, not two,
Especially Dan more careless now of ends,
    More open to the new—
Earth's aim to make more babies, which they did.
Daze nursed them all, then fed them gingerbread.

2

Daze dreamed the world was a tree
With roots invisible and infinite.
    The trunk was life itself
Forever green, all creatures
Were the branches and the leaves, and every twig
    Contained the whole complete
And was contained by all completely whole.
Awake, she lay there wondering in the dark.

3

Her love, her song,
And galaxies turn to that high harmony,
    A rampant wheel within
    A rampant wheel,
As universes veer throughout the void
    Where Daze is burning burning.
Smoke from her fire drifts upward in the night.
We dimly feel it is the Milky Way.

Snakes and Butterflies

1

all happening
Of itself, a loss, a gain
Harassed, unprepared

And always with her
At night chauffered home
To high-rise discomfort

In slums
Alone in a wide worn-carpeted room
Installing a portable shower
All getting sprayed
Seeking help from her
(Go get diploma)
Startling him in a closet
Adjusting his collar of leather
Wishing myself at home
The old bed yet mine

Song building
Where dreams and waking merge
To make a world
Ringing the changes in low play and high
From always deeper down
From always higher up

2

swimming the deep green water
Ecstatically breathing the amniotic ocean
Exploring room by room an aqua castle
Designed by Einstein, built by fish
Convulsing in gold and silver convolutions
Flakes and fluid swirling round my head
Dragged up dripping, gasping for water
Screaming for green and red

I'll show you, said Ann, what Milking Places are.
Here's one. It was a dairy bar
With a molded, modelled horse's hoof and leg
Projecting at an angle below the door of a stall.
You bring your cow in here, said Ann, sit on the bone
      and milk
(It's ride a cock horse and you be the boss)
And fill full many a pail

Then Alma Boffing Boffo said cream was her favorite drink
Heavy cream by Circe beat up in a syllabub

3

 the only one
At breakfast in the cafeteria line
Heaping half-fried fish on top of cold greens
Trying to eat in the desolate hangar room
The cherry pie full of stones
Searching the kitchen freezer
For the non-existent cheese cake

Then she and I went swimming.
I spread the towel on separated boards
Down at the old Boat Harbor
Then edged my way around the tackle house
Where the boat of my childhood, the canvas kayak, sank
When midway round I met a young homunculus
That quickly scrambled over the top
Like a frightened spider.
It was wearing a tiny bathing suit
Bright red, style of 1910

4

that year Detroit decided
To make a few cars of solid diamond
(More or less, the cold blue glare)
And a lady who runs a place here decided to buy one.
It might be a good investment, she said, and I know
My niece will enjoy driving that mother to high school.
It should enhance her self-respect, she said

Harmless and wholesome
That lady's place had little jokes on the wall
Along with pictures of all the local
Politicos and preachers

Her son the bulldog Mayor
He kept this flickering starlet in a glade
And parked his limousine against my creaky Ford
Paint to paint, a joke he said
I'd come to see his girl
Ended by prying the cars apart
Taking off several yards of bleak politician's paint.
She and I drove off in the Model-A

We passed a billboard of raised unreadable letters
Like soft uncertain plastic dentures, Mayan.
Were they from that book of candy letters
Red and yellow jostling each other?

I told her, flickering Alicia, it helps to be
A cross between Mimosa and Rhinoceros.
That ups the survival quotient of an artist
Starlet too

Than live out there with him, she said
I'd rather go down to the gym and sleep on the mats

5

    a bearded magus
Shuffling shards of dung
Till he fashioned a gemmed costume
For Queen Elizabeth in the play.
Is that your vita? we ask him

Aha! he was an artist in a church
Whispering me on how he made his posters
Three cats vertical, just heads
To go for what the union now demanded

Theater to church to courtroom where the lady
Was suing the state for the right to wear
Whatever shade of lipstick she preferred.
Attention! Get attention! was her cry.
Magus and artist shrunk before her screams

I upstairs delaying my descent
Fiddling with toy trains
While in the study the poster maker waited with his wife

Mad at her he cut two holes in her dress
(Having already killed her pet squirrel)
And hung it up by the shoulder blades.
Hung anvils on the hem.
She plays the Queen and forgives him.
We all shake hands

6

a red raw turkey cock
Strutting his feathers of livid flesh

The head of a bird comes out of the mud
Under the water slipping slipping
Neck and shoulders body wings
Up through the ripples into the air
Clanging off in the dazzling noon

We look at the lodge, hot, empty
Listen to singers as the festival starts
Leave and go back to where we are staying
Return on white horses and talk to the singers.
They want to talk about school.
The city is like the city one was raised in
And like a city one never saw before.

A little old lady poet comes from a cocoon
Like a skin-tight toy train
Caterpillaring down a track
To the terminal at the bottom
Thence launching the bard from her nest
In the form of a giant fritillary

White horses of flame
Galloping into the night

7

the first time I played golf
I shot twenty-seven balls
Trying to make the first hole
(I thought you had to do it from the tee)
The fairway was dotted with white
As after a raid from the great Egg Sprayer
That links-eyed haunter of linxes.

The other day I quit on account of my bag.
I noticed I'd stuck all the clubs in head-first
And in there with them I found two flower-pot stands
Jammed together like philosophical gyres, old shoes, old toys
You name it—a cornucopia of all American junk
Gross Gross National Product Inflationary Ooooooze

I stopped right there on the links and went for the car
To pull it up close on the road where I could load it,
Thus to lighten my bag and take a load of balls off
        shoulders already bent.
But someone had stolen the car, and with it my keys.
Even so, I got in and drove home,
Having thrown all that junk in the lake.
I never played golf again

8

professor profile Andy Gump
He was a chiropractor on the side
Happy if I would sub for him
And rub his Saturday patient down
Up in his ramshackle office
In the run-down rotten hotel
While he and his lame assistant
Went to the football game

But first he rose from the floor as Vishnu
Passed through ceiling and attic and roof
Then returned down the chimney as Santa Claus
Without ever once looking back or thinking what
        to do next.

When did Jesus know, said Gump
He was to be the Savior of the world?
When he fell in Eden, said the Lord through Mr. Cayce
From which followed forgiveness of sins
And his love of music because it made silence better

Oh why is Mozart making all that noise?
Pursued by a posse of nuns and clergymen
All later holed up in a gulch, proud of our bodies
Congratulating each other.
White petals of Chopin fall all around us

In a quest for songs undreamed of, never known

9

a leitmotif of feet
From under me beating the floor
Melissa reaching the door now
Calling my name

At the cafeteria she asks for nothing
But mashed potatoes and gravy
(Heap 'em high, she says)
A wrath of a girl subsisting largely on such
Plus Cokes and vitamin pills
The manager's rushing around piling my tray
When ugh I have to leave to keep an appointment
He has to put everything back
(The squash gets mixed with the spinach)

And now I'm driving frantically round in the rain
The dripping umbrella still up over my head
Looking for where I parked the car I am driving
Melissa stands on the curb by a mountainous duffel bag
(It looks like a fallen Cape buffalo)
Waving my furled umbrella in the rain
I have hers, green and too small

I'm never going to make it there on time, I see
We go back in and eat our dinner in peace
All the rushing and striving was for me to take an exam
In an uncongenial subject for which I hadn't prepared

Back to the beef purée and mashed potatoes
With Melissa Lovelady Long, astringent girl

10

skin had always
Been stitched about my organs like that of a baseball
Everyone had such stitches and now my own had worn out
And had to be replaced by my affable surgeon
Whose waiting room was so crowded by others
Also coming apart at the seams

I decided to take a walk and come back later
Walking too far I knew I would never get back
Before closing time unless I ran hard
I tried but the rotten stitches kept breaking
And I kept merging viscerally with the asphalt

Finally holding my sides I caught a taxi
That got me back to the surgeon's office in time
Just barely I asked for anesthesia
Though usually none was required
And the affable fellow complied

With the knife in his hand he saw what a state
I was in and wanted to get the job done
Before he too came apart which he did
Stitching me stitching me
Till I was as good as new and ready to go

I thanked him and made an appointment
For 3:00 p.m. on Tuesday ten years in advance

11

    a black Abe Lincoln mail man
With Che Guevara Black Panther sons
Comes by and asks whatever happened
To your boy's friend Fat Elmer.
He rests his bag on the porch
And introduces his jut-bearded boys

We tell them all about what happened to Fat Elmer

Later I see him in front of a small grocery store
Stacking wood in the trunk of his car.
It's dawn and he tells me he sat up all night
By the fire watching the end of the world on television
Riots everywhere, but there's one more night to go, he says
And invites me over

12

the lout
Clouting the counter out at the airport
Sullenly lurking behind the coffee urn
All-Pro great hero man
I ask my friend if he would like to meet him
He says he already has

The same guy out on the beach shouting at strangers
While Candice and I put rubber rings round our necks
And hit the surf

The fat fellow fighting food in the fish shack
Looked with terror at losel climbing the steps from
        the pier
That fellow's out to get me, he said, stuffing in
        crab ice cream and Coke
The old boys leaned on the weathered bench and laughed
        the losel grinning
And coming on and coming on

Short swagger back from hunting
With his bristly mustache and wire-press clotted with
        birds
His hunting car full of family, children and Grand Pa
Who go with him to the field
But now he says it's back to my desk and study
McSorg McSorg

13

you'll never get
To the second floor if you wait for this elevator
Arriving an hour too late and seated high as Uriah Heep
In a desolate room full of snow, I wrote in elegant
    Renaissance script
On a subject I knew nothing of, renaissancing
Getting it done

Relaxing that afternoon
The paradigm emerging on the pillow
Faulty fruit of body on the bed
Dreaming of Hermes alit by lying camel in the desert
Back arched, arm up, eyes to sky
While Polly crosses thighs and brushes the hair from
    eyes
If I don't get it filled out this summer, I murmur,
    then fall, then spring
They'll hear from me

I tie a knot in a coupling of snakes
That frizz on the floor, whiz-whirr in the tub.
We use them for bait and catch a golden dragon.

That's great, says Polly. Do it, darling, and to
    hell with Hermes and him

14

leaving her with the rest
I walked the back roads of Bimini
(We just call it that)
With stranger met at the dock.
I gave him a chocolate-covered chestnut or two
Peering through vines at a small bearded woman
    nuzzling a child
On the porch of a tiny cottage.

Friend said, These people are Arabs and haunted
By the ghost of
Adam Clayton Hemingway.

Out where the blue was banging the beach
We went to the large museum, saw statue
Of two long lionesses curved tail to tail
The folds in their pelts half making signs
Like a strange old poem.
Read it, he said. I can't, said I.
It's ancient New Zealand script, tougher than Aztec.

Back with her
I like it here. I want to spend the night.
Yes, but if we leave the group
How will we get back to Mainland
In the morning, huh

15

striking
The strumpeted glamour guy under the strobes
He the male starlet dancing it off
I too, weeping to think what we had bought
And had to return to
The perfect bungaloed babied split level
Surrounded by factories fuming and foggy highways,
    O foh!

But not so bad
Having guushy with Margo her thighs running over
She Cardinal Newman's mistress for eleven years
The best most meaningful years of the great man's life
(I'm not romantic, she says. I think science is sexy)
Interruptions. I go in and give
The boys whatfor for making so much racket.
Margo brings in food, a basket of bread and fish, food
That Ruth fixed for Jacob, I tell her

Then out in the car crawling from back seat to front,
    Margo,
I'm still in back. She takes the wheel. I see the car
Full of fashionable Frenchmen coming toward us
On the perilous bridge

There at last, Margo and I
Racking for some excuse to reach the moonlit bushes
Beyond the dance floor, dusty
When Bubbles in velveteen comes over to dance with me.
Margo laughs. We dance.
She tells me she's still at the 54th Street pier,
Bubbly Girl with her lame boy plea for love.

Margo's writing a paper on night-herding ghouls
(They're freckled, Huck Finnish creatures)
Wants to know where she can find out more about them.

Pudgy Boy says he knows. Bubby Girl giggles.
He says he had to get away once
So spent forty days in the mountains
In the Great Smoky fastnesses fasting
Lonely with Little Dog, his lonely only friend.
He said they saw plenty of night-herding ghouls.
Only the lonely see them, he said
They're nice

16

they serve delicious
Gravy before the movie
But only on Sundays. Best
I've ever tasted, she said
Thinned with a beater. We went.
Down the row a man was singing hymns
Old bum who said he knew me
Called me by name. I'd given him
Two hundred dollars, he said
Three years ago in Cambridge

After the movie
We stopped by the bird preserve
Spotted a snowy owl.
I climbed the tree
Trying to catch it. It changed
From owl to egret
From egret to tiny tit
A sliver bird, a splinter
A linkumsluice, a lolly
Whereon the tree went dead
Sapless sere branch broke
I fell to autumn floor
Where Alexandra kissed me, brushed me off
As tiny tit flew far away
With a belly laugh in the woods

17

born among giants, half of them witches
Later inventing gods to take their places, trying
To make them resemble each other

Canned fruit spilled on the sidewalk, guzzled by us
While watching the little black girl singing and dancing
Her crook-faced uncle snatching a pineapple ring
And shaking his fist in my belly, his bright bolt blasting
Nothing

He the old goat man who said that book was the best
For learning to sing Paradise Lost, the one
In white leather soiled with the lady's kid glove
Crumpled up in front. He wandered the woods
Singing Paradise Lost, the bearded black old goat man
Sandalled and sorry

The youth with the gaping wound in his side
Trying to find him, listening for sounds of his
        singing

Then having shot the people from the men's room window
He flushed himself down, gurgling
I couldn't find him
That same ferret-faced fellow surfacing plump in the kitchen
At three o'clock in the morning

108

18

while the puppy
Regurgitated rice loaves larger than he was
The furrowed women looked on with frowning concern
Their husbands all hospitalized with rickets and scurvy

I leave my seat and the puppy at the Noel Coward play
And walk out past the stage to the door behind it
I enter the audience watching and inside Jane and I
Talk, saying we're sorry. Meanwhile her husband
Snaps my picture, says he likes 'em that way, unposed

I left and kicked up my monkey-shine heels in front of
        the church
Then went next door to the parsonage to pick up my tennis
        shoes
Where they'd been waiting for eighteen years, met Jane
The parson's daughter, who turned into sow, me into boar
While heels of the Keds grew wings

Flying us to the cathedral where
Vaguely the Cardinal asked how his baby was doing
Swelling his crest. I'm afraid it's dead, she said,
        smiling.
He quaked and eructated, that ruddy old bird, whistling
Throughout his long scarlet, muttering something anent
The Prots and RC's fighting for dominance, yeah

Then quickly moulted into an old Indian Mage
Somebody 'twixt Nehru and a Brahma bull
Great gray hump across his shoulders, dewlap folds
        hanging down
Glaring back over hump at the drunk college boy
        coming in
Rejecting Jane
While pulling his battered bulk back to his book
        and ballsy cubicle
Hauling his erudite hairy wine skin

19

now sitting in Einstein's lap, saying
How Hitler's not in the best anthologies anymore
He's in this one, said Liz.
Einstein holds the book nose-close.
Humpf, he says, spelling out lines from Mein Kampf
While shadowy girls angling their pelvises forward
     stroll past the blue window

Dear, he chortles, there's a crack, you know, in the
     Liberty Bell
Pushing pelvises, Polly the winner
So to the bar in the kitchen, sitting, talking to
     the glittering ancient
She told how they'd been to the lake, Leelanau, subsisting
     on nothing
But tomato soup and sardines for two weeks

We went down town. She broke her heel
Of transluscent plastic. I met one tall and freckled and
     pale.
You've stopped swimming, I said. Come on over
To Macy's with me and go in their pool
(The brass facade shone dully through the snow)

We stayed at the Fireplace Hotel
In rooms with little unburnable boxes
Me and the glittering crone
With pale Eliza

When it broke, transluscence heeling over,
Don't stop to fix it here, she gritted.
Take my arm, said I, and when it goes completely
Grab me. Fling your arms and cling, O glittering
    dame

Then falling through the theater's floor
Threatening to leave and walk all twenty miles home
(Go ahead, they said)
Falling fear of falling turning into
Jet plane won't take off running lifting into
    into joy of eagles

Belle it, sell it, says Liz. O God, the gas gauge registers
    zero and I, well I just filled it

20

the New York designer
Moved to Main Street, where he lived above a cheap
  restaurant.
When visitors thumbed his sketches and wrecked his work
He slowly turned into a shaman, shrill and transvestite,
To rival Handsome Lake, Short Bull, Beauregard Barefoot,
  and Father Divine,
Empty Wagon and Winnebago Crashing Thunder.

Age of Angst indeed, he cried, when instead of threatening
  bombs
We were off dawn-dauntless to hunt the Wooly Mammoth,
  Giant Aurocks, and Cave Bear
Armed with only a flint-headed spear and empty belly
Our big man having died in his descent
To paint several miles underground, slipped
And washed away

And now an international crisis cult
With every man his own big medicine maker.
While the funky designer now culture redeemer is
  telling the boys a dirty story
I'm wondering why Melissa felt like that
And is she still asleep, as from the murky room I look
Up at her window

21

wearing my silks
On the highways of Europe
Driving a bump car, Alpha Romeo
Eating with friends in a restaurant not ready
Going to do my guard duty in a glowing Halloween mask

The tall girl stands at the head of the line. She wants
    to get in and eat.
I take her with me and dress her up as a bride.
She rides with me in the bump car down the hall
And out through the landscape of France

A turn in the Skyline Drive
And the car was climbing a cave-wet wilderness stairway
Hewn from rock. Terrified I stopped.
We crawled out over the back and spiked our way down.

Next day they had a small fair, where a local loser
Drove the car blindfolded all the way up, turned
It around and drove it back down, having charged admission
And sold via wife and children some hundreds of ice cream
    cones
To the giggling mob of mountaineers

22

and now
What you see is a man going down
Treading the bright anthracite in the sapphire dark
Spreading before him the man-made muddy lake
Huge roots lining the shore, trees dying, fishless
    water
(Thousands of plugs, not one strike, says the Mayor)
Above it a floor, a house for municipal functions
A banquet hall, beyond it a ballroom

I told him I'd once caught a fish and eaten it raw
Loved the blood popping into my mouth

We walked through the place with the party of tourists
Coming out Jane said, God what a ballroom. What a vast
    expanse of man-made muddy nothing
And anyway who could dance above all that dead water?
My God you look awful, she said, as she glanced at my beard
She crucified on her father's corpse who'd worn one
But forbade his sons to do so

Then suddenly up from that lake of dead water rearing
The Brontosaurus. Screaming he shat my embryo out in a
    nest of soft grasses, and died
Yeah, a nest of soft grasses to rest it on

23

this mannish old lady
Says she was born at the Petty Larsen
Turns into Polly Garter
Then into Dumb Dora and Tillie the Toiler.
She wants to go with us and does

She says, I like him. I like him a lot.
I met him walking and smiling, singing
That bed of Rose's that I lay on
And bend her like a fender full of finns

It's not a rat race, buddy, said Betsy. It's a dance.
You understand, and I'm dancing it
(Good God, she sighs, this body! It'll be the death
        of me yet)

Egged on by her
Spearing the passing cars with sharpened two-by-fours
Piercing the fenders
All around us snow and angry drivers
The poles in their holes erect and wobbling
Margo giggles, They have a regular slot in the fenders now
A place to carry their two-by-fours

Oh not that thing, groans Ann, about piercing cold cars
With two-by-fours, oh no
Country cold cars, cold country cars

A ten-degree morning, frost on the moon, a lavender
    sliver near the horizon

And so I promise a happy ending
Hilaritas
In fact you've already had it

Silly and playful
That's it
For words cannot do it, pointers only
So thank ye, O Pooky Punjab
Yeah, thanks

24

the designer back
In New York wouldn't talk and he wouldn't hang up.
He said just enough to keep me there
While he listened to see who else was in the room.
He didn't know, but strongly suspected, I had his
    whole house full of friends

Outside the Captain falls from the sun-whitened pier.
His wife, no swimmer, leaps in to save him.
I crawl from under the house where I'd been checking the
    mail box
Run through the porte-cochere held up by one cedar pole
    at the corner
Dive in and save them both, dragged up dripping
Don't do that again, I say, till you've both had some lessons

And there on the porch was old Sir Richard back from the
    dead
He and Fat Momma complaining about my work.
There're specks on those pears, they say
You could've painted them better

But I'm already inside again and talking with Margo
Asking, Did you go out with Mary Louise while I was gone?
Well, we went dancing, she said. Lord was it dark in there.
But none of the fellows showed.

Really, said Mary Louise. I came home to find Zack
His head bashed in with a hammer. That's right, said Sue
He was running his wife down daily until it happened
She already connected with two disappearances

Meanwhile the giggling Evangelist, frothing, dressed
    in robes of hot pink
Held back by his wife and manager tried to get at her

25

while I
Take your blood pressure again, my son
Peruse this tome of alabaster letters
Called Queen Lear, the work of one of your fellows
A complete re-working and reversal, a re-revamping
     if you please
Of the two Elizabethan drama versions

Going from is to as and back to is again

I hand the book to the shadow who waits behind the counter
Serving us something out of Satyricon
Powdery white wearing only an apron
Which he playfully whips aside, exposing himself

Just as I'm asking Ann to go upstairs
Surrounded by children on tiptoes for her attention
This won't work, so off to the play, the auditorium
Where I relax with colleagues, fellow fellaheen, watching
     the learned Randall slip in the side door
More like through a seam in the wall
Thin and withered, hysterically giggling, he dances down the
     side aisle
Winking at us with a knowing leer at Margo
We all sit back and chuckle

26

immured
In a room with the President, his wife and valet
I open a wall and run but am recaptured

We lie lined up in beds like babies on a maternity
    ward

Morning comes. We make for the three washstands
    in the hall
I, excluded, come back to the room
And try to eat my leather shaving kit.
Give it up. Red leather no go. Too tough. I don't
    have the teeth and stomach for it

Then there're three men swimming the green inland sea
Two crawl-churning ahead, one cross-stroking behind
The women, wife and daughters, left in the boat
The first two reach the beach and climb the high hill
    for beer
I, the third man, gulp the green water and grin
At the President waving
As I throw the sparkling scud behind me with a lash of
    my hair

27

a huge blue
Steel-shafted jet nosing up the avenue
Hovering just off the asphalt, tilting
Into the suburbs, momentarily righting itself, taking
        off
No, failing, coming down flat in the street

There changing to huge diesel truck
With Candice and Polly fighting
To see who'd drive it off.
You lucky bitch, says Polly

Then Candice triumphantly shows me the picture
As all of us sit in the bathroom
The old lady painter ensconced with her husband
Explaining the symbols

I say I like it, but mostly
Am eager to fly or diesel truck it again
Then rush downstairs to breakfast
Brushing past Polly as I round the post at the bottom

The picture's entitled Youth
All three of the girls kept saying how awful it was
I liked it though, with its map-like sections
Its diagrammatic forms in green and orange

28

shouting
I zinged the golfball into the mitt of Fat Momma

Stella leaps and frisks about on the plain
We join her and throw the ball, soccer-size now, back
and forth

Stella says, Come, let's swim
We rush out the 54th Street pier and plunge off the end

Then suddenly there in the sky we see a great horn shining
A scimitar crescent straddled by one of the nymphs, bikini-
clad, from the pier
And under it letters of fire, saying
As long as you're still making it, friend, try us for
perfume and cosmetics

Dry, back out on the plain, again
I zinged the golfball into the mitt of Fat Momma
Stella frisking

29

with Anita
She's filling me in on the new hemlines
At night, she says, hitching her minidress up
I wear it only to here

We go to the terminal building
I take her into the men's room
She sits on the shoe-shine stand
While I sit back by the wall and wait for her
Legs open, thighs, pantyhosed to the dark

She's blonde and smiling
The men who come in aren't as surprised as I am
They grin at me and wink

Then piling the Packard through the greasy gray mud.
Other cars stranded. We try for Trenton. Fail. Back
    out.
I tell Candice never to take that road. Anita agrees
As baffled we stare up the two long tracks in the greasy
    gray mud

30

the fishermen biteless
Brine-broken and hopeless, leap into the water
And beat the bright brine, kicking the depths with
    their bootless feet
Feeling for fish, bumping by fins of silver, bumping
    by flashes of gold

I dive and surface with one in my hands, ten pounds of
    flapping muscle
I heave it up to Mary Louise on the pier, spreading her
    legs
Bracing herself for the action

Always in the woods as a boy, I fishing or walking
She came from the greenery, lithe and lovely
We lay entwined on the moss, in the leaves, beneath the
    tall trees

Now her buttocks spread
On the marble washstand where she sits watching me
    in the tub
I'm standing up washing myself. She stares, runs
For the door, comes back with a cast on her leg
She says, When we try to do it, it swells
It cracks the cast and I dig my heels in his back so
    hard he screams

Then in comes Tillie and drapes her over the tub
Her head goes under the water, long hair floating
She comes up gasping, splashing

We make it better on the scatter rug on the bathroom floor
With the hot water heater clanking away at our feet

Tonight I take her out to the airport and put her aboard
      the great plane
I'd said no, now I want to go
I scrounge the world for a ticket. None's to be had
I wave as she boards the flying cock, long neck and
      golden comb
I wave again as it rockets up in the dark

31

what used to be the Grand Hotel
Is now the President's house at the beach, Buckroe
    Beach on the Bay
I ask him why the thin white layer of dust
Covering the pink brick floor
He smiles an enigma and writes in the dust with his finger

It's Daddy Warbucks in his olive drab slicker in the shower
    with me
Raising his black umbrella

I leave, go into another room
Where I lie with the starlet in front of a fire blue
    blazing white and green
And warm her feet between my lap and the pillow

At last we go out to walk on the beach
We pass through the room where the President sits, bemused
    and idle
We say goodby to him and his wife
Then walk for miles talking with seagulls

32

the little brown cat holds
A full hand of cards, pricking them with her claws
Playing gin rummy. Bridge is next, I say

Then we go out to the wedding at Greenlawn where the
    striped tarpaulins cover the punch bowls
The bride is cavorting with raised naked knees off to
    one side in the shrubbery

At the distribution of goods we're given two infant boys
Non-identical twins, Scandinavian and Latin looking
I thought we were through with all that, I say
With new hope twitching somewhere

But I have to fight Black Bart. He shoots me through
    the heart
I lie with the blood pulsing out through my tattersall
    vest
He leaves me for dead mid the horses. I get up and go to the
    surgeon's office
He makes his probe and pronounces me likely to live

So it's a long voyage for me
With Captain Brenner of the huge luxury liner. Both
    surgeon and sailor
He will not speak the small cabin cruiser that passes
    in front of our bow

We capsize and sink as a great tidal wave goes crashing
    and curling
Over the fields, bearing buildings before it, and me, racing
    the piling foam

33

that afternoon visiting friends
Egypt is merely a mandala shaped laid pattern of bricks
In their backyard, their patio laid by themselves

I say, How disappointing. Margo says, I have to go
Home now and talk with Mother
She takes a bench from the house, now Synagogue
A serpentine bench of loose-linked Aztec letters
And says she'll ride it home

I say, No, don't steal the bench. I'll hail a cab
I fold it up under one arm and take it back to the holy
        museum
Where I throw it down on an old mummy bed under archeological
        eyes

I hail a cab. In the back getting out is the starlet,
        aggressive
Girl! I say, Thank you. She says, Thank *you*! and leaves
Her glove in my hand

If only we could get out to where the pyramids are, I say
I know they'd be more than this. We can take Mother's car
And drive out there on our own, says Margo, watching for
        camels crossing
We do, but during the night the pyramids have vanished
We stare out over the sand

34

and so we came down
From the lake up near the Canadian border
To see how work was coming on Margo's house at the beach

They'd built it out, back and front, and painted it white
Inside renovated, painted, new closets, new shelves
Margo, I say, you should have been with us up there at
    the lake
We canoe across at dawn for those great Canadian breakfasts

Bridget the beautiful insists on ironing me a handkerchief
She's using one of the scaffolds left by the painters
The cord of the iron running between her legs and plugged in
    God knows where

I say, You don't have to do that. She says, I know, but
    I want to

We go outside and walk around the windowless house
The yard is completely sand with pines and poison ivy

We get in the car and wave, heading back for the lake
And who knows

two pink akin holes
Big Rattler's puncture Joe comatose in the dim shed
I'm raising him up

Helping him out the Volkswagen
Should we go down to the station and call Ambulance?
We got him home

I went down and swam in the flood-swollen field

Joe came from his room, didn't even know he'd been bit.
We showed him the holes. He grinned.
The old brain feeding the new brain butterflies, he
      chortled.

That night at the play we talked about
The life of Ben Franklin that both of us were reading.
Joe grinned

And right in the middle of that Eloise sent me a letter
With Phase Him Out scrawled on the back
And inside a picture of the Baby Jesus
And a color brochure of all the stages of life
From embryo on. That's Eloise all right

The fang marks pink like inverted nipples
Sucked on by savage cells

In a quest for songs undreamed of, never known

III

From Fables from Aesop

THE BULL AND THE BUG

A proud little bug crawled up on a bull
For whatever bugs eat when they sup on a bull
And sat on his back until she was full.
When she at last was about to crawl down
From the bull who was big and brawny and brown,
She noticed the bull had a quiet little frown.
So she said, "Mr. Bull, I'm aware of your beef.
You frown because you think I'm a thief.
So I guess it will be an enormous relief
When I've had enough and got out of your hair."
"Why I," said the bull, "didn't know you were there.
I wrinkle my brow, but I really don't care."

THE SNAKE AND THE CRAB

A snake and a crab lived in the same den,
    And the crab was straightforward and lawful,
But the snake was what he had always been—
    Crooked and awful.

The crab kept begging the snake to be
    More honest, and kindly he stroked him,
But the snake was a crook, and finally
    The crab up and choked him.

Then as he saw him stretch out, he said:
    "My friend, why straighten out now?
The time for that was before you were dead,
    When I told you how."

THE FARMER SHUT IN WITH A LION

A lion walked into a farmer's yard
And the farmer, who had for some time tried hard
To catch the lion, shut the yard gate.
But now his surely was a hard fate,
For the lion ran over his milk pails and spilled them,
Then turned on his cattle and sheep and killed them,
Then sprang for the farmer, who now couldn't wait
To let the lion out by opening the gate.
So unless you have something to get a new skin with,
You'd better watch out what you shut yourself in with.

THE DONKEY AND THE BOOK

With many a witty jest and quip
A dog and a donkey were taking a trip
That they had won as a scholarship
When the dog said, "Look!" and suddenly stopped
To pick up a book that someone had dropped.
Then up on the back of the donkey he hopped
To read the book as his friend had suggested.
"Read it out loud," the donkey requested.
"That way a book is best digested.
I'll let you ride as long as you read.
For books, you know, I have a need
That very nearly amounts to greed."
Well the book, it seems, was all about meat
And other things that dogs like to eat,
And some of the pages the dog would repeat.
He read a whole chapter on nothing but bones,
While the donkey twitched and gave little groans
Along with several bored little moans.
"Ah, skip some of that," said the donkey with scorn.
"Perhaps there's a chapter on fodder or corn.
There's a chapter on hay just as sure as you're born."
But no, there was nothing at all about hay
Or fodder or corn, and soon a loud bray
Expressed the donkey's fuming dismay.
"Ah, throw it down here," he said. "It's done
So poorly I feel I can have more fun
Just chewing the paper it's printed upon."

THE TWO CRABS

Once Mother Crab and her daughter
Came up out of the water
To take a walk on the beach.
This was greatly enjoyed by each,
But soon Mother Crab got cross
And said she was at a loss
To know why her daughter walked
So poorly, and Mother Crab talked
And talked, saying, "Daughter, why
Do you keep walking sideways, when I
Have told you and told you, I know,
To walk straight. Now isn't that so?"
"Yes, Mother," her daughter replied,
"You've told me I walk to one side
And that I should walk straight ahead.
All this you've said and you've said.
But I learned to walk from you,
By watching the way you *do*
When you leave the water to walk,
Not by hearing you talk.
And as sure as the beach is wide,
Mother dear, *you* walk to one side!"

THE WOLF AND THE LIONESS

Mrs. Wolf did lots of bragging
   About all the children she had,
And sometimes it sounded like nagging
   And sometimes it wasn't so bad.

But one day a lioness came
   Who had just one little cub,
And Mrs. Wolf called by name
   All her children, to give them a rub.

Then she said to the lioness: "See
   How many nice children are mine.
Here are Willy, Milly, and Lee,
   All washed and fed and fine,

And this one I call Guy
   And this one's name is Brian."
"I see," said the lioness, "I
   Have only one—but a LION!"

THE MONKEY AND THE PORPOISE

A Greek ship bound for Athens was wrecked
By a gale that had sufficient effect
To sink the ship just a few miles short
Of the harbor Piraeus, the Athenians' port.
But the porpoises loved all Athenian folks
And now they hardly at all had to coax
The weary sailors to climb on their backs,
And there they sat like dripping sacks
While the porpoises, filled with porpoise pity,
Carried them safely back to their city.
Now that was the time in Athens when
It was the custom of seagoing men
To take their monkeys and dogs on trips
Whenever they put out to sea in their ships.
So one of these creatures was seen by a porpoise,
Who thinking it human, said, "Hoist your wet corpus
Up on my back, for I'd just adore
A chance to take you safe into shore."
Then quickly the monkey, for that's what it was,
Climbed up on the porpoise, shaking her fuzz,
And there she sat, blinking her eyes,
Drying herself, and looking quite wise.
Said the porpoise, "You live in Athens, of course."
"Oh yes," said the monkey, "no one needs force
To make me claim a city so fair.
My family is likely the oldest one there."
"Well, well," said the porpoise, "surely, then,
You and your famous Athenian kin
Have often gone to visit Piraeus."
"I'll say," said the monkey. "If you could come see us,
We'd take you with us to visit Piraeus.
He's likely the best friend I have in town."
At this the porpoise showed signs of a frown,

Since he knew well that Piraeus was not
The name of a person, but that of a spot—
The spot where ships were kept at anchor.
So looking back at the monkey with rancor,
The porpoise dived and suddenly sank her.
He swam off in hopes of finding a crewman,
Or anything honest and reasonably human.

THE MEN AND THE OYSTER

Two men on a beach discovered an oyster
And one of them snatched it and shook off the moisture.
But it was claimed by the other man too
And neither could make up his mind what to do.
So when a third man happened along
They asked him to judge the one in the wrong
And say to whom the oyster should go.
"Very well," he said. "I think I know,"
And taking his knife he opened the shell.
"Ah yes," said he. "I know very well."
With that he swallowed the oyster down,
And looking at each of the men with a frown
He gravely presented a half shell to each.
"That," he said, as he went down the beach,
"Is justice for all, and don't hold a grudge.
The oyster will cover the cost of a judge."

THE YOUNG MOUSE, THE CAT, AND THE ROOSTER

A young mouse returned to the hole one day
And since it had been his first time away
He had some rather strange things to tell.
"Oh Mother," he squealed, "this day has been swell!
Early this morning I left the hole,
Where all my life I had lived like a mole,
And decided to take a good long stroll.
And oh, Mother dear, you just aren't aware
Of the many marvelous things out there—
Especially two most remarkable creatures.
One was so soft with the gentlest of features,
But the other had none of the good creature's charms,
But raw meat on his head and terrible arms,
And two more pieces of raw red meat
Shook under his chin when he moved his feet,
And then all at once he stood on his toes
And beat his arms like goodness knows!
And screamed so loud I thought I would die—
And just when I was about to try
To introduce myself to his friend.
Oh Mother, I say you just can't comprehend
How nice the other strange creature seemed.
Never before had I even dreamed
That anything earthly could have such fur,
And oh you should hear the gentle thing purr!
In fact, her fur and her ears resembled
Those that we have, and her whiskers trembled."
"My child," said his mother, "from this you can see
How wrong a young mouse can sometimes be.
For the creature you saw with the meat on his head
Was a harmless rooster who soon will be dead

And from whose bones after he has been cooked
We'll nibble all that has been overlooked
By those who will soon make a meal of him.
But many a mouse has been torn limb from limb
And all of our lives are made rather grim
By that other creature that you say is gentle.
That, child, was a cat, who is quite temperamental
And whose favorite food is tender young mice!
Believe me, son, she is so far from nice
That both in the yard and in the house
She's the worst thing there is about being a mouse!"

THE BIG GAME HUNTER

A hunter searching for lion tracks
   In a forest where lions weren't many
Asked a woodsman to rest his ax
   And to say if he had seen any.

"Plenty!" the woodsman replied with good will,
   "And tracks aren't all I have seen.
If a lion is what you're eager to kill,
   I can show you one, tawny and lean."

"Hrrumph!" said the hunter. "Just tracks are my aim.
   Now you can go back to your trees.
In fact, I think you are greatly to blame
   For being too eager to please."

THE OLD TROUT'S ADVICE

A fisherman out on a lake by a mill
Cast his fly with such dexterous skill
That a young trout rushed up, intent on devouring,
But paused when he saw that his mother was louring.
"Stop!" she cried, as she blew a bubble.
"How do you know that fly isn't trouble?
It may be a fly like the ones we adore—
But it may be the kind they sell in the store!
Someone will probably rush up and nab it,
But don't let yourself be that eager to grab it.
Then too, if the fly *is* the good kind to eat,
The first fish to try may meet with defeat.
He'll probably make a splashing big fuss
And drive the thing right over to us."
Just then a young bass who couldn't wait
Shot up from the bottom and swallowed the bait,
Which finished the fish as it did many more.
It *was* the kind they sell in the store.

THE GREAT LEAP AT RHODES

A man who had been overseas for a while
Came home and talked in very high style
Of all his adventures and wonderful fun
And of all the marvelous things he had done.
He told of numerous episodes
But mostly of one—a great leap at Rhodes
That he had made. "You may think I'm plump,"
He said, "but you should have seen that great jump!
I took a good run and leaped through the air
Much farther than any other man there,
So very great is my physical fitness,
And many people in Rhodes will witness
To that mighty leap I made in their city."
"But," said a man, "we don't need a committee
Of witnesses here some three or four deep.
Since leaping is always easy and cheap,
Just pretend this is Rhodes and show *us* the leap!"

THE LION AND THE FOX

A lion too old to have any heart
   For hunting, thought of a trick
Whereby he could eat by playing smart.
   So acting sick,

He entered a cave and waited for callers,
   And this is the way he would greet them:
Since really the cave was baited for callers,
   When they came he would eat them!

But a keen fox stood well out from the cave
   And asked the lion how *was* he.
"Not well," said the lion. "I'm too weak to wave,
   And my tongue is all fuzzy.

I'm really quite sick. Come on in closer."
   But the fox refused with a shout:
"I've seen so many go in, I'll say *No* sir,
   For none have come out!"

THE CROW AND THE CLAM

A crow found a clam on the shore
And tried for an hour or more
There on the beach all alone
To break the shell on a stone.
Then a sly old crow happened by
And decided he'd keep his eye
On the crow who was so plainly
Beating the shell quite vainly.
And soon the old one said, "Friend,
I think I see what you intend.
But let me say this, if I may:
You'll never break it that way.
So take the advice of a crow
Who has lived long enough to know
And after quite high you have flown
Let the clam drop on a stone.
Then the shell will break open wide
And you can eat what's inside.
And after the shell has been broken,
You'll see how truly I've spoken."
So up the younger crow flew,
And when he got high in the blue,
He let the battered clam fall
Without even thinking at all,
And it broke apart on a stone
Where the sly old crow sat all alone.
But before the crow in the sky
Could come down to earth from so high
The old one had pounced upon it
Just as if he had won it,
And then he started to peck fast
And ate the clam for his breakfast.

THE SHEPHERD AND THE SEA

A shepherd drove his flock for grazing
Down by the sea, where he sat gazing
Out on the calm blue water till he
Was seized with an urge to sail the great sea.
So he sold all his sheep and bought a ship,
Which then he loaded with dates for the trip
And set sail at once for a faraway port.
But a terrible storm soon cut the trip short
By sinking the ship along with the dates
As well as the shepherd along with his mates,
But he was lucky and found an old door
To which he clung till it washed up on shore.
Pretty soon after that when again the sea
Was bright and blue and as calm as could be,
One of his friends was admiring it.
"Watch out," warned the shepherd. "That hypocrite
Just seems to be peaceful, as thus she waits.
She looks that way when she's hungry for dates."

THE DOG AND HIS MASTER'S DINNER

A dog had been very carefully trained
  To carry his master's dinner to him,
And daily he did it and never complained,
  Though his own stomach felt a bit thinner to him.

The question the neighborhood dogs all had
  Was what was he carrying in the basket,
And very soon both the good and the bad
  Had run along side of him to ask it.

And once or twice they ganged up and tried
  To run by and snatch his master's dinner,
But he would have fought until he died
  To keep it from harm, and was always the winner.

But one day all of the dogs tried to talk
  Him into giving what they couldn't take,
And when he talked back and slowed down to a walk,
  Right there he made his biggest mistake.

For they made him feel like such a fool,
  He soon dropped the basket and seized the roast beef,
Such as often had made the poor fellow drool
  But had never been able to make him a thief.

THE FOX WHO LEARNED TO DIVIDE

A lion, a donkey, a fox
Together went after the flocks
Since they had agreed to share
Whatever they happened to snare.
When soon they had taken enough,
The lion said, "Split up the stuff,
Mr. Donkey, and see that you're fair."
This last he said with a glare
Which the donkey apparently missed.
All he got was the gist
Of what the lion had ordered.
So he measured what they had slaughtered,
And after a few bad starts
He portioned out three equal parts
And told the lion, "Pick one."
But the lion was hardly a sick one,
And with a fast blow of his paw
He fractured the donkey's jaw
And knocked him head over heels
So far he seemed to have wheels.
Then trying not to sound gruff,
He said, "You split up the stuff,
Mr. Fox, and see that you're fair.
Don't just stand there and stare."
At once the fox made a huge heap
Of all the dead goats and sheep,
And some feet away, for his own,
He put a small lamb all alone.
Then he said to the lion, "Your choice."
At this the lion's deep voice
Took on a note almost pleasant.

"Why I ought to make you a present,"
He said. "It is indeed rare
To find one who knows how to share.
Who taught you how to divide?"
"The donkey," the fox replied.

THE KING AND THE CREATURES

A king decided that he'd give a prize
To the creature best able to criticize
Whatever he thought was wrong with himself.
So he took a gold trophy down from the shelf
And calling them out, he said to the ape:
"Look around you, sir, and try not to gape,
Then say if you're satisfied with your shape."
"Well I should think so," the ape replied,
"And shouldn't I be? Now if *my* hide
Were like Mr. Bear's, all bulgy and saggy
And lumpy and coarse and just plain baggy,
I'm sure that I *would* have something to say."
"Pshaw," growled the bear, "don't talk that way.
I'm fine as silk, but you take our friend
Mr. Elephant there. I could recommend
Some changes in him. Now he's *really* saggy
And lumpy and coarse and bulgy and baggy,
And I hope that he won't think it's a dig
If I say that his ears are somewhat too big.
Then, too, his tail is somewhat too short,
Or so, at least, I've always been taught."
"I'm very well pleased with the length of my tail,"
Mr. Elephant said. "But I think Mr. Whale
Is much too huge to be really good looking.
He must be too fond of Mrs. Whale's cooking."
"Well I," said the ant, "am pleased with all,
Except I'm afraid Mr. Flea is too small.
I rather doubt that he'll ever be
Really big and burly and strong like me."
And so it went for hours and hours,
Each creature using his critical powers
To say what was wrong and even grim

In all of his neighbors but not in him.
"Ho hum," yawned the king, "it's back to the shelf
For this gold trophy for knowledge of self.
No one here will win it today.
I'd a whole lot rather throw it away!"

THE TWO MEN AND THE AX

One day two men, Mike and Max,
Were taking a trip when Max found an ax.
"Look here," he said, "at what *I* have found
Lying out here with no one around."
"Now don't say *I*," said Mike, his friend.
"Say *we* instead, since at least to the end
Of this trip we are on, it would be more kind
For us to share whatever we find."
"Oh no," said Max, "this ax is all mine.
Between *yours* and *mine* let's draw a straight line,
And you'll do well to remember this ax is
Nobody else's at all but Max's!"
So Max took the ax and the two men began
To go on, but soon saw a mean looking man
Who was big and rough and angry, too,
And searching all over for someone who
Had taken his ax from where it was left.
He obviously thought he had lost it by theft.
"Look out!" said Max. "Do you see what I see?
Unless we're lucky, I fear that *we*
Are in for it now!" "That's where you are wrong,"
Said Mike. "Only Max gets the ax. So long!"

THE LION AND THE LEOPARD

A leopard who'd stolen a lamb
Got himself into a jam
While taking it back to his den.
For he met a lion then,
Who offering no excuses
For his uncounted abuses,
Took the lamb away,
Causing the leopard to say:
"You thief! You bully! You fake!
You've no right at all to take
A lamb that belongs to me.
Lambs, you know, aren't free!"
"Oh," said the lion politely,
"I feared you might not take it rightly.
But tell me, Mr. Leopard,
Was this a gift from the shepherd,
Or did you go out on a limb
And buy the lamb from him?
Lambs, you know, aren't free!
I wonder who'll take it from me."

THE PORCUPINE AND THE SNAKES

A porcupine, cold and wet in the rain,
　Was looking for shelter,
And long she looked and looked in vain,
　All helter-skelter.

At last she found a den of snakes,
　Who asked her in,
And when she had gotten over the shakes,
　She was treated like kin.

But the snakes couldn't live with her prickly quills,
　Into which they kept bumping,
And they came to think that of all earthly ills
　She was the most thumping.

So they had to ask the porcupine
　To leave their nice home.
But she had come to like it just fine,
　And she hated to roam.

Said she, "My dear snakes, *you* may go if you wish,
　But I like it here.
Or you can keep coiling around swish swish.
　I've nothing to fear."

THE EAGLE, THE CROW, AND THE BLUEJAY

As king of the birds, the eagle would call
His subjects together each spring and each fall
To have a discussion of things that mattered.
But the crow caw-cawed and the bluejay chattered
Each at the other with so much fuss
That all that anyone there could discuss
Was the quarrel between the bluejay and crow,
Which sounded as if it were going to grow.
And the quarrel was over which one should be first
To make his speech, for both had rehearsed
And now at the meeting each was prepared
To tell all the birds as much as he dared
Of just what things he thought *did* matter.
But now all either could do was chatter,
And each seemed to think that he would be cursed
If he spoke second instead of first.
At last their words took on such a sting
That they had to ask the eagle, their king,
To be their judge and tell them the worst,
As to who should speak second and who should speak first.
Now the eagle thought the whole thing was a joke,
But very seriously he spoke.
"I think," said he, "I know what to do
To end the quarrel between you two.
The first speech will be—and I make this a rule—
By whichever one is the greater fool.
But the answer to this I cannot provide,
So I'll leave it up to you to decide."

THE MOLE AND HER MOTHER

A mole, one day at tea,
Said, "Mother, I'm sure I can see."
Since this no mole can assume,
Her mother got out her perfume
And made her daughter wonder
By putting a little right under
The young mole's velvet nose.
Then as a test she chose
To hold the bottle out
Almost touching the snout
Of the daughter who said she could see.
"Now what do you take this to be?"
Her mother asked the young rebel.
"Oh that's a little wet pebble,"
Her daughter replied at once.
"Ah, my dear little dunce,"
Mother Mole said to her daughter,
"To you perfume is just water,
For you are not only blind,
Which I say without being unkind,
But even your sense of smell
Does not really work very well."

THE WOLF AND THE LAMB

A lamb was drinking downstream
   From a wolf who'd been empty all season,
While the wolf was upstream thinking
   Of what he could use as a reason

For gobbling the lamb. So he growled:
   "Don't muddy my water. Scram!"
Then closer the hungry wolf prowled.
   "Why I'm drinking downstream," said the lamb.

"Well I heard that last year you made
   Some ugly remarks about me,"
Snarled the wolf, and with this he laid
   Back his ears and came closer. "But gee,"

Said the lamb, as the wolf bared a fang,
   "I hadn't been born then." "You're bleating
Just fine," said the wolf as he sprang,
   "Just excuses that you keep repeating—
   But all I'm concerned with is eating!"

One time the frogs were very unhappy
For lack of a leader. "Someone snappy,"
They said, "is all we need to be great,
And we'd rather have him soon than late."
So they sent a messenger up to the king,
Who said, "O king of everything,
We frogs would like a special leader,
A king of our own, and I am the pleader
Chosen to come and ask this of you."
"Very well," said the king. "I know it's true
That creatures feel better with one to obey,
Someone bigger and stronger than they."
So he sent a servant down to the bog
With a fairly bulky old brown log,
And the man threw it in with a splash, and cried:
"Here, O frogs, is a king you can ride!"
But the frogs didn't like King Log a bit.
He was much too quiet and lacking in wit,
And he never gave them any commands
Or sent them away to foreign lands,
Nor did he do anything that was snappy
And calculated to keep frogs happy.
So they complained to the high king again,
Who now lost his patience and sent them a crane,
Who proved very snappy indeed as their leader,
For since he was truly an endless eater,
Every time a poor frog followed him
He snapped him up and greedily swallowed him!

THE CAT AND THE FOX

A fox was bragging one day to a cat
About how smart he was and all that,
Especially at getting out of a fix.
He said, "Why I know a thousand tricks
For escaping the dogs, while you, poor kitty,
Know only one, and that's a pity.
A very smart fox with the dogs—that's me,
But all you can do is climb a tree."
Just then came the hounds with barking and yelping,
And the poor cat truly needed no helping
To climb a tree all the way to the top,
And none of the dogs decided to stop
As after the fox they swiftly ran.
But though he knew a thousand tricks,
None of them got him out of *that* fix.
They caught the smart fellow where none was his friend,
And that, I'm afraid, of him was the end.
But the cat's one simple tree-climbing plan
Worked as well as any plan can.

THE CLOWN AND THE FARMER

It happened one year at the county fair
That everyone liked a clown who was there,
And he, after getting some loud guffaws,
Would then get a round of loud applause.
But most of all they appreciated
An act in which he imitated
The grunts and squeals of a little pig.
Then the applause was really big.
He would act as if a pig were concealed
Beneath his coat whenever he squealed.
But no pig was there, of course, as he proved
At the end of the act when his coat was removed.
Now a farmer present could not help but frown
At so much attention paid to the clown.
So he challenged the fellow to a squealing contest,
And the next day all came with unusual zest
To see who would win, the clown or the farmer.
The clown squealed first, and was such a charmer
They clapped till their hands began to burn.
Then at last the farmer got his turn,
And taking his stand upon the stage
He pretended to grunt and squeal with rage,
But under his coat where he gave it a dig
He really did have an angry pig,
And the noise he seemed to be making with feeling
Was really the sound of a real pig squealing.
The people, however, were not impressed,
And all said the clown had won the contest,
Whereupon the farmer produced the pig.
But it was *his* surprise that was big,
For the people showed great ingratitude
As loudly they hissed him and threw things and booed.

THE ELEPHANT'S SPEECH

A wise old elephant hoped to move
All of the creatures to change and improve.
So he got up at one of their meetings,
And after the usual grunts and greetings
He gave a long sermon in which he spoke,
For over an hour without one joke,
On how improvement was their greatest need,
Since they were so full of hatred and greed.
Now some of those listening liked what he said.
The innocent dove often nodded her head.
The industrious ant and the diligent bee
Clapped and clapped with the greatest of glee,
As did the obedient camel and sheep.
But Mr. Ape was fast asleep,
And when he did wake up he mocked
The way the elephant swayed and rocked.
And the tiger was tired and the wolf was bored
And the wasp and the hornet actually snored.
The scornful fly made a scornful face
And the grasshopper hopped right out of the place.
"Alas," the elephant said in the end,
"I had hoped you would all take advice from a friend,
But I see that the only ones who will heed it
Are those who I'm happy to say don't need it."

THE THIEF AND THE INNKEEPER

One time a thief took a room in an inn
Where very soon, he thought with a grin,
He'd find a valuable something to steal.
But nothing he found there had much appeal
For a thief like himself, except one thing,
And that indeed was fit for a king—
A beautiful coat that the innkeeper wore
Whenever he sat outside by the door.
So one day the thief went out and sat
By the innkeeper's side and started to chat.
But soon long shadows came over the lawn
And the thief reared back with a terrible yawn,
For as he yawned he gave out a howl
Like that of a wolf who is out on the prowl.
"Egad!" the innkeeper cried with alarm.
"Why do you howl so? Do try to be calm."
"All right," said the thief, with a pitiful whine,
"And I will explain this howling of mine,
But first, I beg of you, hold my coat,
For it is a garment on which I dote
And I'm afraid I'll tear it to pieces.
You see, just as soon as my third yawn ceases
I really turn into a wolf and attack
Whoever's around, from the front or the back."
So saying, he howled out yawn number two,
And the innkeeper started to leave for Peru,
But the thief took hold of *his* coat by the collar
And said, "Don't leave. I'll just try to follow
And get you to hold my coat for me."
And with that he howled out yawn number three,
Whereat the innkeeper was so terrified

He slipped from his coat and ran off to hide
Some place in the inn where the wolf couldn't find him,
Gladly leaving his coat behind him.
Meanwhile the thief, who was also a liar,
Made off with the coat that had been his desire.

THE DOVE WHO WAS LOOKING FOR WATER

A dry and dusty dove
    Noticed a painted picture
Of water with clear sky above
    Hanging from a hidden fixture.

And since she thought it was real,
    She took a somewhat absurd path
Right through the window to steal
    A very inviting bird bath.

But the picture she hit with a crash,
    And instead of falling in water,
She fell in a basket of trash,
    Where a little boy soon caught her.

THE DYING LION

A lion whose days of power were past
Lay down in a field to breathe his last
When by came a boar, and seeing him so
He dealt the lion a terrible blow
With his gleaming tusks, thus paying him back
For a wound he had got in an old attack.
Then a bull charged in with lowered head
And gored the old lion, now almost dead.
Pretty soon a donkey, who'd viewed with alarm
The attacks on the lion, saw that no harm
Had come to either the boar or the bull.
So since with sheer spite he was very full,
He trotted up to where the lion lay
And blurted out an insulting bray.
Then backing up to within a short space,
He gave the old king a kick in the face.
"Ah," groaned the lion, "the bull and the boar
Were just about all I could take, and more,
Though they at least are powerful creatures.
But now for an ass with no admirable features
To kick me when I am unable to rise
Makes wretched life a thing to despise."
And the next day he died, but with a smile,
For all of a sudden, in royal style
Three young lions, followed by more,
Sprang on the donkey, the bull, and the boar,
Who had fully expected that they would live on
After the ailing old lion was gone.
But things were no longer as they'd been of yore,
And instead of after, they died before.

THE EAGLE AND THE FOX

An eagle with little eagles to feed
Saw just exactly what they would need—
A little cub of smart Mother Fox
Playing hopscotch down there on the rocks.
But when she swooped down and caught the poor cub,
The other small foxes raised such a hubbub
That Mother Fox came and looked up in the air
And begged the big eagle if she would please spare
The little fox that Mother Fox loved.
But the eagle by this was not a bit moved,
For she knew *her* babies were high in a tree
Where no Mother Fox was likely to be.
So she carried the cub to her little ones,
Who would eat anything that wriggles or runs.
But just as they were going to eat,
Mother Eagle felt breeze of unusual heat,
And looking she saw the source of her scorch—
Mother Fox below with a huge blazing torch!
For instead of standing and wringing her paws,
She'd run to a fire and caught in her jaws
A big blazing stick, and now with great zest
She threatened to burn the tree and the nest.
But this was too much for the eagle, and she
Screamed, "Stop! I beg you. Don't burn up this tree.
To bring the cub down is my only desire—
Just do something else with that horrible fire!"

THE SNAKE'S TAIL

The tail of a snake was always rebelling
Against the head, fussing and yelling
Because the head always went first.
"Of all positions, mine is the worst,"
Shouted the tail. "I'm *really* cursed.
In fact, I'd just as soon be dead
As always be dragged along by a head!"
The head argued back and tried to explain
That the tail had no eyes, that the tail had no brain.
But the tail was stubborn, and talk was in vain.
So one day the head got tired of the nagging
And said, "All right, *you* do the dragging.
You go first and do your worst.
I'll follow behind and keep on wagging."
Then off they slid at a breakneck speed,
For which there wasn't the slightest need,
But, as the head had again to explain,
The tail was without a trace of a brain.
Even so, for a while they did fairly well,
Though what happened next is painful to tell.
For they came to a cliff, craggy and high,
And since the tail had no sign of an eye,
Over they went and not at all slow
And landed FLAP! on the beach far below.
And with them they carried the lengthy middle,
Whom they regarded as sort of a riddle
And whom neither head nor tail had consulted
Regarding the dangers of just what resulted
From letting the foolish tail go first.
But still the snake did not suffer the worst,
For though he went FLAP! on the beach, nothing burst.
He just had his wind knocked out for a while,
And when he slid off the head wore a smile.

THE MOUSE AND THE BULL

When a mouse ran over the back
    Of a bull that slumbered,
He might have been stuck by a tack
    The wild way he lumbered.

But the mouse darted into a hole
    That ran through a wall,
Which the bull with no self-control
    Tried hard to make fall.

He'd stand off and run and butt it,
    Bellowing loudly,
But though he managed to cut it,
    The wall stood proudly.

Then through the hole came the snout
    Of the mouse, who was grinning,
And this he said to the lout
    Whose head was now spinning:

"You big ones don't win them all,
    Mr. Bull, as you see.
Sometimes it's good to be small
    And tricky like me."

THE WOLF AND THE CRANE

A wolf with a bone in his throat
Requested help from a goat,
But the goat was unable to aid him.
He then met a crane and paid him
To pull the bone out with his beak.
So the good crane first took a peek,
Then stuck his whole head down the gulf
That yawned past the jaws of the wolf,
And before his patient could groan
He pulled his head out with the bone.
But the wolf, without a kind word,
Took back his pay from the bird.
"You ought to be thankful," he said,
"That you, friend, still have a head,
Having had it so deep in the jaws
Of a wolf with teeth like a saw's!"

THE WISHFUL BEACHCOMBERS

Two men were walking along a beach
When one saw something far out of reach,
But riding the waves in toward the shore.
"Look!" he cried, "there're riches galore,
Coming our way in a great ocean ship
Heading home from an overseas trip.
I'd bet anything it's loaded with treasure
And other fine things to give people pleasure."
But as it got closer, the other said, "No,
From the way it's rocking to and fro,
It's hardly a treasure ship at all.
It's a fisherman's boat with this morning's haul
Of good fresh fish. And who could want more
When lunch is so near down here on the shore?"
And as the object came nearer and nearer
It also became dearer and dearer
To both of the men who watched from the sand.
When at last it had nearly washed up on the strand,
One of them said, "Oh, we were both wrong.
It's a great long chest, from maybe Hong Kong,
Or some place like that, lost from the deck
Of some good ship that went down in a wreck!"
With that they each plunged into the ocean,
Both possessed by a single notion—
To get to the long dark object first,
And they tried so hard they nearly burst.
But all the thing turned out to be
Was a big but worthless old water-soaked tree.

THE MOON AND HER MOTHER

The moon once said to her mother,
"I hope it won't be any bother
For you to knit me a coat
So when through the sky I float
I'll look more stylish all night,
And please make it fit me right."
"My child," her mother replied,
"You'd never be satisfied
With any coat I could knit you,
Since no coat at all would fit you.
For nothing, not even your name,
Is ever exactly the same.
You change all the time, my daughter,
From full to half to quarter,
And you, since brighter when bare,
Look better with nothing to wear."

THE TWO MEN AND THE BEAR

Two men agreed to do all they could
To help each other get through a wood
Where lots of bears were said to be.
But when a bear came, one man climbed a tree,
While the other, unable to get away,
Fell down in the path, and there he lay
As still as he could, as if he were dead.
Then the bear came up and sniffed round his head,
And almost killing the poor man with fear,
He gave him a lick or two on the ear.
But the bear lost interest and went off to beat
About in the bushes for something to eat,
Since bears don't care for meat that looks dead.
Then the man came down from the tree and said:
"Ha, ha! old fellow, what did the bear say
When he whispered into your ear that way?"
"Why," said the other, "he said that whenever
I go through this forest, I surely should never
Go with a friend who is so afraid!
That's a mistake I should never have made."

THE LION AND THE BOAR

One hot summer day a lion and a boar
Angrily met with a grunt and a roar
At a very small spring that was known to be fickle
And from which that day ran only a trickle,
Enough for one, but not for two,
So grunt and roar was all they could do.
For each had worked up a really big thirst
And each was determined that he would drink first.
Then just as they started a furious fight,
The lion looked up and saw a bad sight—
A big flock of buzzards circling around
To see what would happen down there on the ground.
For they were ready to eat either beast.
Whichever one fell would be something at least,
Or better still, if both should fall
There'd be enough meat to feed them all.
"Look there," said the lion. "Frankly I think
I'd rather for you to go on and drink
Than for us to do what I think we might
And wind up as buzzard meat after this fight."
"I quite agree," grunted the boar.
"Why should we fight while buzzards keep score?
So let us try to share with no fuss,
Before they fly down and try to share us!"

THE DONKEY WHO DIDN'T CARE

An old man out in a field of clover
Was grazing his donkey, when suddenly over
The top of a hill came a whole band of thieves
With pistols in belts and knives up their sleeves.
"Run, my donkey," the old man cried.
"We'll try to find a good place to hide."
But the donkey just kept on munching the grass.
"Tell me," he said, "if it should come to pass
That I am taken by those bad men,
What do you think would happen then?
Would they make me carry any worse load
Than you make me carry out on the road?"
"Why I suppose not," the old man replied.
"But hurry, my donkey, we really must hide!"
"You hurry, old man. Go hide in a cave.
I've nothing to gain and nothing to save
By running away from the men coming yonder.
You see I am not a single bit fonder
Of you than of them, so long as they
Don't double my load or give me less hay."
So the donkey stayed and was caught by the thieves,
Who doubled his load and fed him on leaves.

THE EAGLE AND THE BUG

An eagle pursuing a rabbit
But still unable to grab it
Heard the voice of a bug
Whom the rabbit was trying to hug,
Since the bug was the only protection
She could find in any direction.
"Mrs. Eagle, please!" said the voice,
"Make a more merciful choice
And spare a bug's dear friend
Whose life is not ready to end."
But no, the horrible eagle
Said, "I'm too busy to haggle,"
And right before the bug's eyes
She ended the poor rabbit's cries
And ate her in front of the bug
Without so much as a shrug.
She thought the bug was too little
To do anything worth a twiddle.
But later the bug did her best
To find the big eagle's nest,
And every time there were eggs
The bug would tuck in her legs
And spreading her wings she would whirr
Up high to where the eggs were.
Then since she still bore a grudge
One by one she would nudge
The eagle's new eggs from where
They would go sailing down through the air
End over end to crash
With a great big golden splash,
And soon there wouldn't be
A single egg in the tree.

Mrs. Eagle got more depressed
With each year's empty nest,
But no matter at all where she hid it,
Still the bug did it and did it.
So the eagle few to the queen,
Who was always ugly and mean
To everybody but birds,
And after they'd had a few words,
The queen said, "Here's what we'll do.
You lay your eggs in my shoe.
We'll warm and hatch them there
While I wear another pair."
So the eggs were carefully kept
By the bed in which the queen slept.
But the bug got wind of the plan,
And hiding in the queen's fan
The bug was carried to bed
Into which she leaped unafraid,
And then all through the night
The bug did nothing but bite
So that by morning the queen
Was feeling exceedingly mean,
And leaping out on her legs
She forgot all about the eggs
And stuck her foot in the shoe,
Turning eagle eggs into glue.

THE FISHERMAN'S LUCK

A man rowed out in the ocean to fish,
Hoping to satisfy a strong wish
To make a big catch, and out there for hours
He tried and tried, using all of his powers,
But he was so far from catching a batch
That not one single fish did he catch.
At last, worn out, he decided that there
Just weren't any fish, and gave up in despair,
And since nothing else occurred to him then,
He sat for a while before going in.
And while he was sitting, with nothing to do,
Out in the water there came cutting through
A large and wildly excited sailfish
Being pursued by some kind of whale fish,
And leaping he landed right in the man's boat,
Which he had some trouble keeping afloat,
So big was the fish that came through the air
While he was just quietly sitting there.

IV

From the Iliad and the Odyssey of Homer

From The Iliad

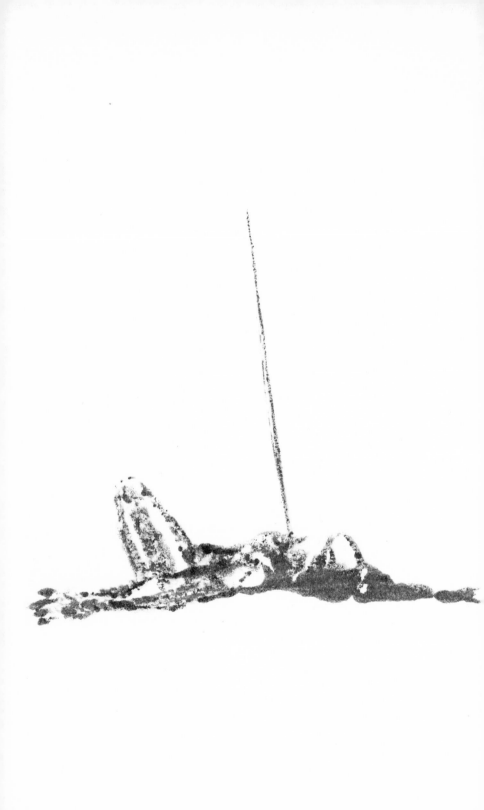

THE QUARREL

Then swift Achilles, scowling at Agamemnon,
Answered him thus: "You greedy-minded shamelessness
Incarnate! how can any decent Achaean want to
Take orders from you, to go where you tell him to go
Or battle his best with hostile men? I didn't
Come here to fight because of the Trojan spearmen.
They've never done me any harm, never rustled my cattle
Or horses, or plundered in fertile Phthia a harvest
Of mine, for between here and there lie a great many things—
Shadowy mountains and crashing sea. But we
Came here with you, the incredibly shameless, in an effort
To gratify you! to get satisfaction for Menelaus
And you! covetous cur that you are. All this
You turn your back on and choose to forget, and now
You threaten to take my prize of prestige, the gift
I got from the sons of Achaeans and for which I labored
So much. Whenever we warriors sack a populous
Trojan city, my share of the booty is never
Equal to yours. True, I get more, much more,
Than my share of chaotic battle, but when it comes
To dividing the loot, your portion is always far larger
Than mine. Worn out with fighting, I go back to my ships
And with me take some pitiful little prize
Allotted to me—little, but mine. Now, though,
I'll go back to Phthia, for I would much rather take all
My beaked ships and go home than stay on here in disgrace
To heap up wealth for you!"
              And the king of men
Agamemnon answered him thus: "Go on and run,
If you feel the urge so strongly. I do not beg you
To stay on my account. I've others here
Who honor and respect me, including the best of all counselors,

Zeus himself. Of all the god-nurtured leaders,
You are most hateful to me, for strife is always
Dear to your heart, and battles and fighting. And if
You're so full of valor, that's the gift of a god.
So take your ships and your men and go lord it over
The Myrmidons at home. I have no regard for you,
Nor do I care how angry you are. But see now
How you like this. Since Phoebus Apollo is taking
Chryseis from me, I'm returning her with a ship
And men of mine—but I myself will come
To your lodge and take your prize, the lovely Briseis,
That you may know for sure how greatly I
Exceed you in power and excellence, and another man
Will think twice before calling himself my equal and right
In my presence comparing himself with me!"
    He spoke,
And the pain from his words went deep in mighty Achilles,
Rending the heart in his shaggy breast two ways
As to what he should do, whether to draw the sharp sword
By his thigh, break up the meeting, and kill Agamemnon,
Or else to swallow his rage and control his temper.
While he was thus divided in mind and heart,
With that huge sword of his half drawn from the scabbard,
Pallas Athena came down from the sky, sent
By white-armed Hera, the goddess whose heart held equal
Love and concern for both of the angry men.
Standing behind him, she caught the raging Achilles
By a handful of tawny hair and made herself visible
To him alone, nor could any of the others see her.
Astonished, Achilles turned, and as he looked
In the blazing blue eyes of the goddess he knew her at once
For Pallas Athena, and his words came winged with surprise:

"Why, O daughter of aegis-bearing Zeus, do you come again
Now? Can it be that you wanted to witness the hubris
And gross overreaching of Atreus' son Agamemnon?
Well let me say this, and believe me I mean what I say.
That arrogant pride of his may shortly cost him
His life!"
    And the bright-eyed goddess Athena replied:
"I came down from the sky to help you control
Your wrath, if only you will obey, and the goddess
White-armed Hera sent me, for her heart holds equal
Love and concern for both of you. So come,
No fighting, and don't draw your sword. Wound him with words
Instead, and tell him just how it will be. And now
I say this to you, and I too mean what I say.
On account of this arrogant insult, splendid gifts
Worth three times as much as what you may lose will one day
Be given to you. So hold yourself back, and obey us."
    Then Achilles, swift of foot, answered her thus:
"No man, O goddess, can ignore the word of two
Such powers, no matter how wrathful his heart may be.
To obey is surely better. The gods hear all
The prayers of him who heeds them."
                        He spoke, and restrained
His mighty hand on the silver hilt. Then obeying
The word of Athena he thrust the long blade back into
The scabbard. And the goddess left for Olympus and the palace
Of aegis-bearing Zeus, to mingle with the other gods there.

                                        (From Book I)

HELEN

Meanwhile Iris arrived
With a message for white-armed Helen, and she came in the likeness
Of her sister-in-law Laodice, the loveliest daughter
Of Priam and the wife of lord Helicaon, son
Of Antenor. Helen she found in the hall, weaving
A web of double width and of iridescent
Purple. And in it she wove not a few of the battles
That the horse-breaking Trojans and bronze-clad Achaeans had
        suffered
At the hands of Ares on her account. Standing
Close by her side, nimble Iris spoke to her, saying:
        "Come, my dear, that you may see an incredible
Thing that the horse-breaking Trojans and bronze-clad Achaeans
Have done. They who but lately were eager to clash
On the plain and tearfully tear each other to pieces
Have now called off the battle and are sitting quietly
Out there, leaning back on their shields, with their long spears
        fixed
In the ground beside them. But Paris and fierce Menelaus
Are to use their long spears to fight each other for you,
And you will be called the dear wife of whichever one wins."
        These words of the goddess aroused in the heart of Helen
An irresistible yearning for her former husband,
Her city, and parents. Quickly she veiled herself
In shining white linen, and softly crying hurriedly
Left her chamber, not by herself but attended
By two of her handmaids, Aethra, daughter of Pittheus,
And heifer-eyed Clymene. And quickly they came in sight
Of the Scaean Gates.
        There in the council of Priam
Sat the elders of Priam's people, Panthous and Thymoetes,
Clytius, Lampus, and Hicetaon, scion of Ares,

And two other men of wisdom, Ucalegon and Antenor.
Too old for battle, these elders were excellent speakers,
And now they sat on the wall like forest cicadas
That sit on a tree and sing with their lily voices.
Even so, the leaders of Troy sat on the turreted
Wall, and when they saw Helen approaching spoke softly
One to another in these words winged with wonder:
      "Surely no one could blame either side for suffering
So much and so long for such a woman, for she
In appearance is terribly like an immortal goddess!
But still, though lovely she is, let her go home
With the ships and not be left here as a curse to both us
And our children."

                                        (From Book III)

HECTOR AND ANDROMACHE

Resplendent Hector reached out to take his son,
But the baby cried and clung to the fair-belted nurse,
Afraid of the way his own father looked, with all
That bronze and the horsehair crest dreadfully waving
On top of his helmet. This made them both laugh, his father
And lady mother, and quickly resplendent Hector
Took off his helmet and laid the dazzling thing down.
Then he took the baby and kissed him, bounced him a bit
In his arms, then prayed this prayer to all of the gods:
    "O Zeus and you other immortals, grant that my son
May be, like myself, outstanding among the Trojans,
As strong as I and as brave, and a mighty ruler
Of Ilium. And may it be said of him someday, as home
He comes from battle, 'There goes a much better man
Than his father.' Let him be bearing the blood-stained bronze
Of an enemy slain, and may he rejoice the heart
Of his mother."
    He prayed, and placed the child in the arms
Of his wife, and she held him close in her fragrant bosom,
Laughing and crying at once. Seeing her so,
Her husband felt deep compassion, and gently caressed her,
Saying:
    "Poor haunted one, do not be overly
Anxious. No man in the world can hurl me to Hades
Before my appointed time comes. And no man, valiant
Or vile, can escape his fate ordained, once he's been
Born. So go to the house and keep yourself busy
With the loom and spindle, and see that your maids are busy.
War is for men, my dear, for all men here
In Troy, but most of all for me."

(From Book VI)

192

ACHILLES AND PATROCLUS

While the others were warring around the benched ships, Patroclus
Came up to Achilles, Prince of his people, and standing
Beside him shed hot tears, weeping like a spring
Whose dark streams trickle down the rocky face of a cliff.
And noble Achilles, a warrior fast on his feet,
Had compassion on him, and spoke in these winged words:
     "Why are you weeping, Patroclus, like some little girl
That runs along by her mother and begs to be
Taken up, clutching her dress, holding her back,
And looking tearfully up at her till at last
She is taken up? Like that little girl, Patroclus,
You shed these big tears. Have you something to say to the
     Myrmidons
Or to me myself? Have you alone heard some late news
From Phthia? Surely men say that Menoetius, son
Of Actor, still lives, as does King Peleus, Aeacus'
Son, at home among his Myrmidons. Were either
Of those two dead, then indeed we would greatly grieve.
Or is your sorrow for Argives, now being slaughtered
Beside the dark hulls on account of their own overreaching?
Keep it in no longer. Speak out, and share it with me."
     Then heavily sighing, the horseman Patroclus replied:
"O Peleus' son Achilles, far strongest of all
The Achaeans, do not mock or blame me for this,
So awesome now is the terrible pain in which
The Achaeans are toiling. For now our bravest men,
Stricken by arrows or spear-thrusts, lie at the ships.
Strong Diomedes, Tydeus' son, has been hit,
And both spear-famous Odysseus and King Agamemnon
Have suffered disabling spear-wounds, and Eurypylus too
Is out with an arrow deep in his thigh, and about these
Our surgeons of many drugs are busy, trying

To help them. But what, Achilles, can anyone do
With you? May wrath like that you cherish never
Lay hold of me, O man perversely courageous!
What profit will men yet to be have from you, if now
You refuse to keep from the Argives shameful destruction?
O creature without compassion, surely you are
No son of Thetis and knightly Peleus. Only
The gray salt-sea and the beetling cliffs of stone
Could have brought into being a creature so harsh and unfeeling!
But if your heart is set on escaping some dire word
From Zeus, revealed to you by your goddess mother,
Then send me forth now at the head of the Myrmidon host,
That I may be a light of hope to the Danaans.
And let me strap on my shoulders that armor of yours,
That the zealous Trojans may take me for you and quickly
Withdraw from the fighting. Then the battling, war-worn sons
Of Achaeans may have a chance to catch their breath—
Such chances in battle are few—and we who are fresh
May easily drive, with little more than our war-screams,
The exhausted Trojans away from the ships and the shelters
And back toward the city."
　　　Such was his plea, poor childish
Fool that he was, for it was his own hard death
And doom for which he pleaded.

(From Book XVI)

ACHILLES AT THE TRENCH

> Then Zeus-loved Achilles
> Got up, and about his great shoulders Athena flung
> The bright-tasseled aegis, and round his head the fair goddess
> Drifted a golden mist, from which she made blaze
> A high-flaming fire. And as when smoke billows up
> From a distant island-city beleaguered by foes,
> And the soldiers defend it throughout the day from the walls
> Of their town till at last the sun sets and the signal fires, many
> And large, send their glare high up in the sky, that men
> On neighboring islands may see and come in their ships
> To ward off destruction, so now from the head of Achilles
> The blaze went up toward heaven.
>   Striding out from the wall,
> He took his stand by the trench, though he did not join
> The Achaean troops, since he had respect for his mother's
> Strict command. He stood there and shouted, while out
> On the plain Athena joined her voice with his, and he caused
> Unspeakable chaos among the Trojans. His voice
> Rang out as piercingly clear as the scream of a trumpet
> When soul-wrecking foes are attacking a city. And when
> They heard Achilles' brazen voice, the hearts
> Of the Trojans were stunned with surprise, and even the mane-
>   tossing
> Horses sensed fear in the air and turned back their cars
> In panic. And their drivers were terrified when they saw
> The unwearying fire blaze up with such awesome glare
> Above the head of great-souled Achilles, for the bright-eyed
> Goddess Athena made the flames rise. Three times
> Across the trench great Achilles mightily shouted,
> And three times the Trojans and their world-famous allies
> Were thrown into chaos. And there twelve men of their bravest
> Were killed by the cars and spears of their own fellow soldiers.

Meanwhile, the thankful Achaeans dragged Patroclus
From under the missiles and lifted him onto a litter,
While round him followed his dear mourning friends, and with them
Went fast Achilles, shedding hot tears, as now
He looked down on his faithful friend, torn by the mangling
Bronze and borne on a litter. He had sent him with horses
And car into battle, but never again did he welcome him
Back from the fighting.

(From Book XVIII)

THE DEATH OF HECTOR

      Fast Achilles, ceaselessly running, pressed hard
Upon Hector. And as when a hound in the mountains jumps
The fawn of a deer and chases him hotly through glade
And winding gorge, relentlessly tracking him down
Whenever he cowers in hiding beneath a dense thicket,
So Hector now could not escape Achilles.
As often as he endeavored to make a dash
For the lofty Dardanian Gates, hoping his fellows
Above on the wall might cover his effort with showers
Of shafts till he gained the protection of well-built bastions,
Achilles would cut him off and turn him back
Toward the plain, while he himself continued to run
On the city-side of the course. And as in a dream
A man is unable to chase one who wishes to flee,
And both, though struggling to run, remain rooted fast,
So that neither gains on the other, so now Achilles
Could not overtake Hector, nor could swift Hector
Escape. But how did the Trojan manage to keep
Away for so long from the fierce fates of death? Only
With help from Apollo, who came for the last and final
Time to inspire him with strength and quicken his knees.
And Achilles signaled his men with shakes of his head
Not to hurl their bitter missiles at Hector, lest someone
Else might win the glory of bringing him down,
And he himself come second. But when for the fourth
Time around they reached the fair fountains, Father Zeus
Lifted his golden scales and set on the pans
Two fates of forever-sad death, one for Achilles
And one for horse-breaking Hector. Then by the middle
He took the balance and raised it, and down all the way
To Hades' house sank the death-day of Hector, whereat
Apollo left him. But bright-eyed Athena came up

To Achilles and spoke to him these winged words:
"Now, finally,
Zeus-loved resplendent Achilles, I've hope that we two
Will cut Hector down, no matter how hungry for battle
He is, and bear to the ships great glory for all
The Achaeans. For now he cannot escape us, not even
If far-working Phoebus suffers tremendously for him
And grovels in his behalf before Father Zeus
Of the aegis. So take your stand and get back your breath,
While I go persuade your quarry to fight with you
Man to man."
So spoke Athena, and Peleus' son, gladly
Obeying, stood where he was, leaning upon
His bronze-bladed shaft of ash. Athena left him
And came up to shining Hector, assuming the form
And weariless voice of his brother Deïphobus. Standing
Beside him, she spoke to him these words winged with beguile-
        ment:
"Dear brother, surely fleet-footed Achilles has sadly
Abused you, chasing you thus around Priam's city.
But come, let us now stand against him and beat back his charge
Together."
To which great Hector, his bronze helmet flashing:
"Deïphobus, you've always been my favorite brother
By far, of all the sons that were born to Priam
And Hecuba. Now, though, I'm sure I shall hold you dearer
Than ever, since you have dared to come out and help me,
While all the others stay back of the lofty walls."
To him then the goddess bright-eyed Athena replied:
"Dear brother, believe me, our father and queenly mother
And all of the comrades about me earnestly pleaded
With me to stay where I was, so fearfully do

They all tremble before Achilles. But my heart was deeply
Pained by piercing sorrow for you. So now
Let us charge straight at him and fight, nor let there be
Any sparing of spears, that we may know at once
Whether Peleus' son is going to cut us both down
And carry our bloodstained armor back to the ships,
Or whether he shall go down beneath the bronze point
Of your spear."
     With these guileful words Athena induced him
To fight, and when they got within range of each other,
Huge Hector, his bronze helmet flashing, spoke first to Achilles:
"No longer, O Peleus' son, will I flee before you,
As I have done three times around the great city
Of Priam, without the heart to stand up to your charge.
For now my spirit says fight with you face to face,
Whether I kill or be killed. Come then, let us
Invoke our gods to sanction this pact between us,
For they will witness and guard our covenant best.
If Zeus allows me to outlast you and rob you
Of life, I'll do to your corpse no foul defilement.
But when I have stripped off your armor, Achilles,
I'll give your dead body back to the host of Achaeans—
And you do the same for me."
     Then savagely scowling
At him, fast-footed Achilles replied: "Hector,
You madman, don't stand there babbling to me of covenants.
There are no faithful oaths between lions and men,
Nor do wolves and lambs have any oneness of heart,
But they are always at fatal odds with each other.
So too it is not to be thought that we can ever
Be friends, nor shall there be any peace between us
Till one or the other has fallen and glutted with blood

199

The battling Ares, him of the tough hide shield!
Recall every jot of your warrior's prowess, for now
Is the time to show your courage and skill as a spearman.
Escape for you there is none, but Pallas Athena
Shall soon bring you down with this long lance of mine.
And now you shall pay all at once for the grief I endured
For my comrades, whom you in your raging killed with the spear."
　　So saying, he poised his long-shadowing spear and hurled it,
But shining Hector, looking straight at him, escaped,
For he saw it coming and crouched, so that the bronze point
Flew over his head and embedded itself in the earth.
But Pallas Athena snatched it up, without
Hector's knowledge, and gave it back to Achilles. And Hector,
His people's commander, spoke thus to the great son of Peleus:
　　"You missed, O godlike Achilles. It seems that Zeus
Has not yet informed you concerning the day of my doom,
Though surely you thought that he had. You thought by your
　　　　glibness
And cunning of speech to fill me with terror of you
And completely deprive me of courage and strength. But you'll not
Plant your spear in my back as I flee, but as I
Charge down straight upon you, drive it clean through my chest—
If God has granted you that. Look out now and avoid,
If you can, my keen-cutting bronze. Here's hoping you take
The whole shaft into your hard flesh! Surely this war
Would be lighter for Trojans, if you, their greatest scourge,
Were dead."
　　Then poising his shade-making spear, he cast,
Nor did he miss, but struck full upon the shield
Of Achilles, from which a long way it rebounded, enraging
Hector, since his swift shaft had flown from his hand
In vain. And now, since he had no second ash spear,

200

He stood in deep consternation, then shouted to him
Of the dazzling white shield, Deïphobus, asking a long spear
Of him. But he was nowhere around, and Hector,
Aware now of just what had happened, spoke thus:
       "So be it.
Surely the gods have summoned me deathward. For I
Thought sure that the hero Deïphobus stood right behind me,
Whereas he is safe on the other side of the wall,
And Athena has tricked me. Now evil death is at hand
For me, not far off at all, nor is there any
Way out. Such, I believe, has always been
Zeus's pleasure, and that of his far-shooting son Apollo,
Who have in the past been willing and eager to help me.
Now, though, my doom is surely upon me. But let me
Not die without a huge effort, nor let me dishonorably
Die, but in the brave doing of some great deed
Let me go, that men yet to be may hear of what happened."
       So saying, he drew the keen blade that hung by his side,
A sword both heavy and long. Then bracing himself
He charged at Achilles, plunging upon him like some
Huge high-flying eagle that dives through dark clouds to seize
On the plain a tender lamb or cowering hare.
Even so, Hector plunged, his sharp sword held high. And Achilles,
Seething with savage wrath, met the advance
With one of his own, protecting his chest with his intricate,
Exquisite shield and tossing his head, so that all
The gold plumes that Hephaestus had thickly set in the crest
Of the four-horned helmet shook with a gorgeous glitter.
And from the bronze point of the spear that Achilles balanced
In his right hand there went forth a gleam like that
Which glints amid stars in the blackness of night from Hesperus,
Fairest of all the stars set in wide heaven.

Hefting that powerful spear, he scanned the form
Of his foe to find the spot where a spear was most likely
To pierce the firm flesh of Hector. He saw that his armor
Of bronze covered him all the way, the beautiful
Gear he had stripped from mighty Patroclus when he
Cut him down. But there where the collarbones separate neck
And shoulders, there at his throat, most fatal of targets,
Appeared a spot unprotected by bronze. So there,
As on him he charged, great Achilles drove in his spear,
And the point went through his soft neck and stuck out behind.
Even so, the ashen shaft, heavy with cleaving bronze,
Failed to sever the windpipe. Hence Hector could still say words
And answer his foe. Dying, he sprawled in the dust,
And shining Achilles exulted above him, vaunting.

(From Book XXII)

PRIAM AND ACHILLES

Then Achilles called for handmaids
To wash and anoint the dead Hector, bidding them do it
Where Priam could not see his son, for Achilles feared
That his guest might not be able to hold back his wrath,
And so he might lose his own temper and kill the old man,
Thus sinning against Zeus's law. When the handmaids had
      washed
The body and rubbed it with oil and put about it
A tunic and beautiful cloak, Achilles himself
Lifted it onto a bier and helped his companions
Lift it onto the wagon. Then groaning, he called
On his precious friend by name:
      "Do not be angry
At me, O Patroclus, if even in Hades' halls
You hear that I've given Prince Hector back to his father,
For not unbefitting at all was the ransom he gave me,
And you may be sure of getting your due share of that."
      So spoke great Achilles, then went back inside and sat down
In his richly wrought chair by the opposite wall from Old Priam,
To whom he spoke thus: "Your son, old sire, has now
Been released to you as you have requested and lies
On a bier, and you yourself shall see him tomorrow
At daybreak while carrying him away—but let us
Not neglect supper, for even the lovely-haired Niobe
Ate, though her twelve children all died in her palace,
Six daughters and six lusty sons. Shaft-showering Artemis
Brought down the daughters, while Phoebus Apollo put arrows
Through all of the sons with his silver bow, both of them
Wrathful with her for comparing herself with their own mother
Leto, Niobe saying that Leto had only
Two children while she herself had borne many. So they,
Though only two, destroyed all twelve of hers.

203

And there for nine days they lay in their blood unburied,
For Cronos' son Zeus turned all of the people to stones.
On the tenth, however, the heavenly gods held the funeral,
And Niobe, weary of weeping, remembered to eat.
And now somewhere mid the crags in the desolate hills
Of Sipylus, where, men say, the nymphs go to bed
When they tire of dancing about the stream Achelous,
Niobe stands and, though solid stone, broods
On her god-sent disasters. So come, my royal old sire,
And let us likewise remember to eat, and later,
Back in your city, you may lament your dear son
With innumerable tears."
    So saying, Achilles sprang up
And slaughtered a silvery white sheep, which his comrades flayed
And made ready in every detail, skillfully cutting
The carcass into small pieces, which meat they spitted
And roasted well, and drew it all from the spits.
Then Automedon served them the bread, setting it forth
In exquisite baskets, while swift Achilles apportioned
The meat, and they reached out and ate of the good things before
    them.
But when they had eaten and drunk as much as they wanted,
Priam, descended of Dardanus, sat there and marveled
At mighty Achilles, thinking how huge and handsome
He was, a man in the image of gods everlasting,
And likewise Achilles marveled at Priam, looking
Upon his fine face and listening to what he said.
When both had looked on each other enough, old Priam
The godlike spoke thus:
    "Show me my bed, now, Achilles,
O nobleman nurtured of Zeus, that we may enjoy
A night of sweet sleep. For never once have my lids

Come together in sleep since my son lost his life at your hands,
But always I've mourned, miserably brooding on
My innumerable sorrows and groveling in dung on the ground
Of my high-walled courtyard. Now, though, I've tasted some food
And drunk flaming wine. Till now, I had tasted nothing."

He spoke, and Achilles ordered his comrades and handmaids
To place two beds in the portico and cover them
With fine purple robes, light spreads, and fleecy warm blankets,
And the girls went out with torches and made the beds.
Then Achilles, fast on his feet, spoke to King Priam,
Somewhat bitterly saying:

"My dear aged friend,
You'll have to sleep outside, since one of the counselors
Of the Achaeans may come to consult me, as often
They do, and as they should. But if one of these
Were to catch sight of you through the fast-flying blackness of
        night,
He might very well go straight to King Agamemnon,
Commander-in-chief of the army, and so there would be
A delay in my giving back the body. But come,
Tell me frankly. How long would you like for the funeral rites
Of Prince Hector, that I myself may hold back from battle
And keep back the others also?"

And the godlike old King:
"If you really want me to give noble Hector his full
Funeral rites, this, O Achilles, is what you could do
To help me. You know how we're penned in the city and also
How far the terrified Trojans must go for wood
From the mountains. Let us, then, mourn for him in our halls
For nine days, then burn him and hold the funeral feast
On the tenth, and on the eleventh build a barrow
For him. Then on the twelfth we'll fight again,
If we must."

205

To which fleet-footed, noble Achilles:
"So be it, my ancient Priam, just as you wish.
I'll hold back the battle for all the time you request."
     So saying, he clasped the old King's right wrist, in a gesture
Of friendly assurance. Then there in the porch of the lodge
The old ones retired, the herald and Priam, their hearts
Ever thoughtful. But Achilles slept in one corner of the spacious,
Strongly built lodge, and beside him lay Briseis,
Lovely of face.

(From Book XXIV)

From The Odyssey

MENELAUS AND HELEN

So spoke the King, and Asphalion, a zealous retainer
Of illustrious Menelaus, poured water over their hands,
And they helped themselves to the good things spread out
 before them.
But Helen, daughter of Zeus, had other ideas,
And as soon as she could she put a powerful drug
In the wine they were drinking, a sweet and soothing nepenthe
To make one forget all pain of body and mind.
Whoever drank of a bowl in which this was mingled
Could not for one whole day shed a single tear,
Not even if his mother and father lay dead before him,
Nor if he should see his brother or own dear son
Put to the sword. Such soothing and subtle drugs
Had been given to the daughter of Zeus by the wife of Thon,
Polydamna of Egypt, for there the grain-giving earth
Is most fruitful of herbs that are used in the mixing of drugs,
Many quite helpful and healing, many quite deadly.
There all are versed in medical lore far beyond
What other men know, for they all claim descent from Paeëon,
The gods' own physician. Now, having drugged the wine
And made sure that everyone's goblet was filled, Helen
Once again spoke to her husband:
    "Son of Atreus,
God-kept Menelaus, and you other sons of worthiest
Men, Zeus, in whose power all things are,
Gives good and ill to us as he sees fit,
And now surely is the time to sit in these halls
And feast and enjoy the telling of tales. Already
I think of a story that fits the moment well.
It's true I cannot begin to tell all the toils
And achievements of enduring Odysseus, but what a deed
That strong man did at Troy, where you Achaeans

Suffered so much, when he with disfiguring blows
Marred his own flesh, clothed himself in rags
Too vile for a slave, and walked through the hostile city,
Up and down the wide streets, disguised as a beggar, a far cry
From what he really was among his own people
At the ships of the Achaeans! So dressed he entered the city,
And not one of the Trojans knew him. Only I saw through
The disguise. But when I questioned him, he cunningly
Tried to evade me, till finally, having bathed him and rubbed him
With oil, having dressed him and sworn a great oath that I
        would not
Reveal his name to the Trojans until he got back
To the huts and swift ships of the Argives—only then
        would he tell me
In any detail what the Achaeans were planning.
Then, after slaying many Trojans with his long bronze blade,
He made his way back to the Argives loaded with information
And left a city full of wailing women.
But I was glad, for already my heart was longing
To go back home, and I groaned for the stupid infatuation
Aphrodite gave when she caused me to leave my own
Dear country, my child, my marriage chamber, my husband,
A man with far more than his share of good looks and good sense."
    Then tawny Menelaus replied: "All this, my dear,
You have told us justly and well. And truly, though I
Have traveled much about the wide world and known
The minds and hearts of many resourceful men,
I have never seen anyone else so completely dependable
As dauntless Odysseus. Think what he did and endured
In the carved and polished horse when all of us Argive
Leaders sat with him there bearing fateful death
To the Trojans. It was then, my dear, that you arrived—

It must have been by command of some god who wished
To magnify greatly the glory of Trojans—and with you
Godlike Deïphobus. Three times you walked around
That hollow horse and ran your hands over the wood,
And you called out the names of the Danaan chieftains, making
Your voice like the voices of their wives back home in Argos.
I sat with Tydeus' son and great Odysseus
There in the midst of those men and heard you call,
And both of us were eager to get up and leave,
Or right away to call out in answer, but Odysseus
Restrained us, and though we insisted he held us back.
Then all the other sons of Achaeans sat quietly,
With one exception—Anticlus, who alone seemed determined
To call out an answer to you. But quickly Odysseus
Clapped his strong hands tightly over his mouth
And held him so, until Pallas Athena led you
Away, and thus he saved all the Achaeans."
        Then finally thoughtful Telemachus spoke to the King:
"Zeus-nurtured Menelaus, son of Atreus and leader
Of your people, so much the heavier his loss to us,
Since none of this could save him from grievous destruction,
Nor could have, though his heart had been of iron. But come,
Show us our beds, that we may rest in sweet sleep
And forget our troubles."
        Now Argive Helen told
Her maids to place two beds in the portico and cover them
With fine purple robes, light spreads, and fleecy warm blankets,
And the girls went out with torches and made the beds.
Then a herald showed the guests where they were to sleep,
Telemachus the Prince and the glorious son of Nestor,
There in the portico of the palace. But the son of Atreus
Slept in the innermost room of the lofty house,
And beside him lay long-robed Helen, loveliest of women.

                                              (From Book IV)

NAUSICAA

The good Odysseus crept out from beneath
The bushes and with his great hand reached into the thicket
And broke off a leafy branch to hide his nakedness.
Then on he went like a bold lion of the mountains
Who goes through wind and rain with his eyes of fire
In search of cattle, sheep, or wild deer, and when
His belly bids him right into the close-barred fold
To attack the flocks therein. Even such was the need
Of Odysseus as he went in his nakedness to approach that party
Of girls with hair so beautifully braided. And to them
He appeared very terrible indeed, all encrusted with brine
As he was, and they scurried in all directions mid the jutting
Banks of sand. Only Alcinous' daughter
Remained. Made brave by Athena, who took the fear
From her limbs, she stood and faced him, while Odysseus tried
To decide whether he should embrace the lovely girl's knees
And so make his plea, or stay where he was and softly
Beseech her to give him some clothes and show him the city.
Thus pondering, he decided to stay where he was and speak softly
To her, since she might take offence at his embracing
Her knees. So without more delay he spoke these shrewd
And gentle words:
     "I implore you, O Queen—but are you
Goddess or woman? If you are a goddess, one
Of those who rule the wide sky, then surely in grace
Of face and figure you're most like Artemis, the daughter
Of almighty Zeus. But if you're a mortal, one
Of those who live here on earth, thrice-blessed are your father
And fortunate mother, and thrice-blessed your brothers are too.
I can well imagine the wonderful warmth and joy
You give them as they watch so lovely a flower taking part
In the dance. But happiest of all will be that man

Who wins you with the gifts of a wooer and takes you home
As his wife. For never before have I seen such a mortal
As you, whether man or woman. I gaze, completely
Astounded. Once indeed in Delos I saw something like you,
A lovely young palm shooting up by Apollo's altar—
In Delos, where I had gone with an army on a journey
Very rich in misfortunes for me—even so, when I saw
That tree, I marveled long in my heart, for never
Has there been such another curving up from the earth. As I look
At you now I feel that same amazement, an awe
That keeps me from clasping your knees, though terrible
          are the things
That have happened to me. Just yesterday I came out
Of the wine-dark sea after nineteen days of high wind
And waves that bore me from the island Ogygia. Now
Divine power has marooned me here to suffer I know not
What, for surely the gods have plenty of evils
In store for me yet. Have pity, O Queen, for you
Are the first to whom I have come after all my suffering
And toil, nor do I know any of the others who own
This land and this city. Give me some rag to put on—
An old wrapper from the laundry will do—and show me the city.
And as for yourself, may the gods grant all the desires
Of your heart—a husband and home and a wonderful oneness
Between you, for nothing is better or greater than a home
Where man and wife are living harmoniously together,
The envy of evil minds, but a very great joy
To men of good will, and greatest of all to themselves."
          Then the white-armed maiden replied: "Stranger,
               since it seems
That you're neither evil nor stupid, this misery of yours
Must be the will of Olympian Zeus himself,

213

Who gives happy fortune to men, whether good or bad,
To each as he sees fit. So you must, of course,
Endure it. But now that you've come to this land and city
Of ours, you shall not want for clothes or anything
Else that a wayworn castaway needs for his comfort.
I'll show you the city and tell you who we are.
This is the country and city of the Phaeacians,
And I am the daughter of great-hearted Alcinous, upon whom
The people depend for all the strength they have."
        She spoke, and called to her ladies with the beautiful braids:
"Hold on! my friends. Since when do you run at the sight
Of a man? Surely you didn't think he would harm us.
That man doesn't live, nor shall he ever, who could come
Bearing malice to this land of Phaeacia, since the immortal gods
Love us too much for that. And besides, we live
Far out in the billowing sea, the remotest of men,
And no other mortals have any designs on us.
But this is some unlucky wanderer, and we must take care
Of him, for all strangers and beggars are surely from Zeus,
And a kindness that we think small is not so to them.
So come, my ladies, find food and drink for our guest
And bathe him in the river in a spot that's sheltered from
        the wind."
        At this they stood for a while and urged one another,
Then seated Odysseus in a sheltered spot, just as
The royal daughter of great-hearted Alcinous had said,
And beside him for clothes they laid out a tunic and cloak.
Then they gave him the golden flask of soft olive oil
And urged him to bathe in the stream that ran by them. But he
Had this to say:
        "Ladies, stand back over there
While I wash the brine from my shoulders and rub my body

With oil, as I haven't done for so long. I'll not
Take my bath in front of you, for I'm ashamed
To be naked in the midst of such young and lovely-haired ladies."
      Thus he spoke, and they all went over and told
The Princess. Now gallant Odysseus scrubbed off the brine
Which was caked on his back and broad shoulders, and from his head
He scrubbed the scurf of the barren and unresting sea.
When he had finished his bath and rubbed himself
With the oil, he put on the clothes which the bride-to-be
Had provided for him, and Athena, the daughter of Zeus,
Made him seem taller and better built and caused
His hair to curl like the hyacinth in bloom. As a craftsman
Who learned his art from Hephaestus and Pallas Athena
Overlays silver with gold and produces a work
Full of charm, so the goddess shed grace on the head and shoulders
Of Odysseus. Then he went over and sat on the beach
By himself, resplendent with masculine charm, and the Princess,
Admiring him greatly, spoke thus to her fair-haired companions:
      "Listen, my ladies. I have something to tell you.
This man's arrival among the godlike Phaeacians
Was not without the will of all the gods
Who live on Olympus. At first he seemed to me
Rather crude and unattractive, but now he looks like one
Of the sky-ruling gods himself. I would like to have
Such a man for my husband here in Phaeacia, and I hope
He decides to stay. But come, my ladies, get food
And drink for our guest."
      Quickly her ladies set food
And drink in front of the noble, long-suffering Odysseus,
And he fell to ravenously, for he had not tasted food
In a very long time.

(From Book VI)

THE CYCLOPS

Odysseus spoke to them, saying:
"Here then is the plan that seemed to my mind the best.
There by one of the sheep-pens lay a great club
Of green olive, which the Cyclops had cut to cure and carry
With him. To us it seemed as long and thick
As the mast of a broad-beamed black merchant ship, a vessel
Of twenty oars that crosses the sea's great gulf.
From this I cut a log about the length of a fathom
And gave it to my comrades, asking that they dress it down
And bring it to a point, which they did, and I myself
Finished the point and thrust it in the blazing fire
To harden. Then with all care I hid it beneath
A pile of manure, of which that cave had its share.
And I asked my men to cast lots to determine which ones
Should have the courage to help me lift the log
And plunge its point into the eye of the Cyclops
Sweetly sleeping. Four men were chosen by lot,
The very four that I myself would have picked.
    "At sunset he returned with those fat flocks
That bore such splendid wool and quickly drove all
Of them into the huge cave. Either from some
Foreboding or at the command of a god, he left
Not a single one outside in the great stockade.
Then he lifted the tremendous door-stone high in the air
And set it in place, sat down himself and milked
The ewes and bleating goats, and placed the lambs
And kids beneath their mothers. This done, once again
He snatched up two of my men and ate them for supper.
Then I approached and spoke to the Cyclops, with an ivy
Bowl of dark wine in my hands:
    "'Cyclops, here,
Drink this bowl of wine, now that you've finished

Your meal of human flesh, that you may know
What kind of drink we had with us in our ship.
I was indeed bringing it to you as an offering,
Hoping that you would take pity and set me once more
On my homeward way, but you have made yourself
Unbearable to us. After such barbarous cruelty,
How can you expect any man ever to visit
You here again?'

    "He took the bowl and drained it
At a gulp, and finding it sweet and greatly to his taste
He asked for more:

    "'Let me have another.
Offer it gladly, and tell me your name right now,
That I may give you a gift that will, I believe,
Delight you. Here the grain-giving earth and rain
From Zeus produce some winy rich clusters, but you
Have tapped the gods' own supply of ambrosial nectar.'

    "So again I handed him the fiery bowl,
And then again, and thrice he foolishly drained it.
When he began to grow groggy, I spoke to him
In a pleasant voice:

    "'Cyclops, you ask my name,
A famous name, and I will tell it to you,
That you may give me the friendly gift you promised.
Nobody is my name. They all call me Nobody—
My mother, my father, and all the rest of my friends.'

    "Then ruthless as ever, he answered: 'Nobody I'll eat
Last of all, and all the others I'll eat before Nobody.'

    "With this he reeled and fell on his back, his thick neck
Bent to one side, and all-conquering sleep overcame him.
As he lay in that sodden coma, he began to vomit
And out came wine and chunks of human flesh.

I took the pole and thrust it deep beneath
The red-hot coals, and with cheerful words I encouraged
All my companions, that no man might flinch when the time came.
Soon that stake, though green, began to glow
A terrible red, as if it would blaze any moment.
I took it from the fire, and as my men gathered around me
A god inspired our hearts with tremendous courage.
Then they took that pointed pole of glowing green olive
And plunged it into his eye, while I bore down
On the shaft from above and spun it around. Like a man
With a drill who bores a ship's timber while those below
Keep the drill constantly spinning with the thong they hold
On either side, so we took that pole with the head
Of fire and spun it about in his eye, and the burning
Blood oozed out around it. As the eyeball sizzled
And its roots crackled, his lids fell completely away,
And his brow began to blister. As when a worker
In bronze dips a large ax or adze into cold water
To temper it and a great hissing is heard—
For iron at least is strengthened by dipping in water—
Even so his eye hissed around the green olive pole.
Horrible were the screams that rang from wall
To rocky wall, and we shrank back in terror.
He tore the stake from his eye, all dripping with blood,
And frantically hurled it away. Then, throwing himself
Wildly about, he shouted as loud as he could
To the neighboring Cyclopes, who lived out there in caves
Among the windy mountains. Hearing his cry, they came
From all sides, and standing around the cave they asked
What his trouble was:
      "'What unbearable pain,
Polyphemus, makes you cry out and keep us awake

218

In this fair and peaceful night. Is somebody rustling
Your flocks or actually killing you by force
Or some trick?'
        "Then from the cave came the voice of powerful
Polyphemus: 'O friends, Nobody is killing me
By a trick, not force!'
        "And they answered with winged words:
'If you are alone and nobody is hurting you,
You must be sick, and sickness you cannot escape
Since it comes from almighty Zeus. You had best pray
To Poseidon, our lordly father.'
        "They had their say
And left, and in my heart I laughed to think
What a sharp trick Nobody had pulled with an improper name.
        "The Cyclops, groaning in agony, groped for the door-stone,
Removed it, and sat there himself with his arms extended
Lest anyone try to get out with the sheep, so stupid
He apparently thought me. But I was searching my brain
For a plan, that my men and I might escape that death.
Many were the schemes I considered, as anyone would,
In the face of that great evil, and here is the plan
I preferred. There in the cave were woolly fat rams,
Great beautiful beasts with fleece as dark as the violet.
I tied them side by side in groups of three
With pliant branches that the lawless monster used
For a pallet. Beneath each middle sheep rode one of my comrades
With a beast on either side for added protection.
As for me, I chose the very best ram in the flock,
And grabbing two handfuls of hair I curled myself up
Beneath his shaggy belly, where I clung in dead earnest,
Holding on for dear life, my face in his marvelous fleece.
Thus with many groans we waited for morning.

"As soon as rosy young Dawn arrived, the rams
Made for the pasture, while the females, their udders bursting,
Bleated unmilked about the pens. Their ailing
Master ran his hands over the backs of the rams
As they passed before him, but foolishly failed to check
Beneath the woolly beasts where my men were riding.
The ram I had chosen started out last of all,
Bearing his weight of wool and my anxious self,
And powerful Polyphemus felt along his back
And spoke to him thus:
      "'Tell me, old fellow, why you
Are the last one out of the cave. It's not like you
To lag behind. You were always the first
To reach the tender grass, practically galloping,
And always the first to reach the running streams,
And always at evening you were the most eager to return
To our home. But now you're the very last one. I believe
You are grieving for the eye of your master, blinded by a horrible
Man and his despicable friends, by Nobody,
Who plied me with wine, and who, believe me, has not yet
Escaped death at my hands! If only you could understand
And talk, you could tell me where he is hiding. Then
I would scatter his brains all over the floor of this cave,
And so relieve my heart of the weight of woe
That no-good Nobody has caused me.'
      "With this he let
The ram go, and when we had got just a little outside
The enclosure in front of the cave I first freed myself
From under the ram and then untied my friends."

(From Book IX)

THE GHOST OF ANTICLEA

"My mother
Approached and drank of the cloud-black blood. She took
One look at me and then in tears she spoke
These words so winged with woe: 'My child, how did you
Find your way while still alive to this
Dark kingdom of gloom? It is not easy for the living
To see these things, for between your world and ours
Lie mighty rivers and terrible torrents: Oceanus
First, which no man can wade. Truly yours must be
An excellent ship. Have you and your friends been wandering
All this time? Do you come here from Troy
Without having reached your home in Ithaca, and haven't you
Seen your wife in all these years?'"

    "And I answered:
'Mother, this trip I had to make, down
To the house of Hades to hear the truth from Theban
Tiresias. For as yet I haven't come near the land
Of Achaea, nor have I set foot on my own island.
But ever since that day when I with glorious
Agamemnon left for Troy to fight the Trojans,
I have been woefully wandering. But tell me truly,
What fate of dateless death brought you so low?
Was it some lingering illness, or were you slain
By the painless arrows of Artemis the archer? And tell me
Of those I left behind, my father and my son.
Do they or some other man receive the honor
That used to be mine, and do they say that I
Shall never return? Tell me too of how
My wife has managed and what she intends to do.
Has she stayed with her son and kept unceasing watch,
Or has already the best of the Achaeans made her
His wife?'

"To this my mother's ghost replied:
'I assure you that her patient heart remains
Within your palace, where pitifully she weeps, as the days
And nights waste slowly away. But the high esteem
That you enjoyed has been given to no one else,
Though Telemachus is undisputed lord of the lands
You own and is invited to feasts by all men
As an equal of any, which is as it should be for one
Who gives the law. Your father, however, lives
Out in the country and never comes to the city.
He has no bed with sheets and soft bright blankets,
But all winter long he sleeps, as would a slave,
In ashes by the fire and clothes himself in rags.
When summer comes and the teeming autumn, his beds
Of fallen leaves are scattered everywhere throughout
His fruitful vineyard. There on the slope he lies
In sorrow, and the grief in his heart is great and growing
As he yearns for your return. His is a heavy
Old age. Even so, death came at last for me.
For the painless arrows of the keen-eyed archer goddess
Were not my fate, nor was my strength, as is
The common lot, destroyed by disease. But longing
For you, for your quick mind and gentle heart—
That surely took my honey-sweet life away,

    "When she had finished, my hesitant heart made me long
To embrace her, and thrice I went toward the ghost of my mother
With outstretched eager arms, and thrice she flitted
Through them like a shadow or a dream. The pain in my heart
Grew increasingly keener, and, when I spoke, my words
Came winged with anguish:
    "'My mother, why don't you wait
For me, since I am so eager to hold you close,

That even here in the house of Hades we two
Might embrace and give full vent to our cold lamenting?
Are you a mere image that mighty Persephone has sent
To mock me and make me lament and groan all the more?'
    "Soon then she answered: 'Alas, my child, unluckiest
Of men, Persephone, daughter of Zeus, does not
Deceive you, but this is the way it is when one
Is dead. For the nerves no longer knit the flesh
And bones together, since the heat of blazing fire
Consumes the body as soon as the white bones are lifeless,
And the soul takes flight like a dream. Now quick as you can
Go back to the light, and remember all these things,
That someday you may tell them to your wife.'"

(From Book XI)

THE BOW OF ODYSSEUS

Quickly, quietly Philoetius went out of the house
And barred the gates of the high-walled yard. Under
The portico lay a curving ship's rope, made
From fiber of byblus, and with this he tied the gates tight
And went back inside. He took the same seat as before
And kept his eyes fixed on Odysseus, who now was handling
The bow, turning it round and round and trying
It out in various ways, making sure that worms
Had not eaten into the long horns while its owner was absent.
Then a young suitor would glance at his neighbor and say:
"Aha! no doubt an old hunter—and filcher—of bows.
Or perhaps he's got some just like it at home. Either that
Or he wants to make one himself, judging from the way
He turns it around and around in his hands, evil
Old tramp that he is!"
And another of the proud young lords
Would say: "I wish the fellow just as much luck
As he ever has success in stringing that bow!"
So they mocked him, but resourceful Odysseus weighed
The bow in his hands and examined it all with care.
Then, with as little effort as a skillful bard
Employs when about a new peg on his lyre he strings
The gut of a sheep and makes it fast at both ends,
Odysseus now, with equal ease, strung
The great bow. And holding it in his right hand he tested
The string, which gave back a musical twang as sweet
As the voice of a swallow.
At this the wooers grew ill
And their faces turned pale. Zeus, by way of a sign,
Gave out a loud clap of thunder, and long-suffering, noble
Odysseus rejoiced at this omen from the son of Cronos,
Crooked in counsel. All but one of the arrows

224

Were still in the hollow quiver—arrows soon
To be tried upon the Achaeans. But now Odysseus
Picked up the swift shaft that lay there bare on the table
Beside him, laid it on the bridge of the bow, and drew back
The string and notched arrow. Then he shot with sure aim
      straight ahead
Without even leaving his seat, and not one ax
Did he miss. In at the first handle-hole, clean through,
And out at the last it flew, burdened with bronze.

                                       (From Book XXI)

THE DEATH OF ANTINOUS

Now able Odysseus stripped his limbs of their rags
And sprang to the ample threshold, bearing the bow
And quiver full of swift arrows, which he poured out there
At his feet, and spoke these words to the wooers:
    "At last
This final tough test is ended, and now I'll shoot
At a mark which no man ever has hit, to see
If Apollo will grant me that glory."
    With this he sent
At Antinous a sharp and bitter shaft. Now that
Young lord had a lovely two-handled cup in his hands
And was just on the point of raising it up to drink
Of the wine. He had in his heart no thought of death,
For who at a feast would ever suppose that one man
There among many, even though he were very strong,
Could bring on him dark doom and evil death?
But Odysseus' well-aimed arrow went in at the throat,
Clean through his soft neck, and the point stuck out behind.
He dropped the cup and slumped to one side, as a thick rush
Of blood came up through his nostrils, and he, with a quick
Convulsive kick of his foot shoved the table away
And spilled all the food on the ground, where bread and roast meat
Were bedabbled with blood. At this the clamoring wooers
Broke into a panic, leaped from the chairs, and ran
Through the hall, scanning the solid walls for weapons,
But not one shield or doughty spear was there
To lay hold of. So they screamed at Odysseus these furious words:

"You'll have to pay dearly, stranger, for making a man
Your target! No more contests for you—your death
Is now certain! To say the least, for you have killed
The best young man by far in all Ithaca.
The vultures will pick your bones right here in this island!"
    Thus the bewildered wooers, who thought he had killed
The man by mistake. The poor fools did not know that they all
Had reached the end and were now bound fast in the bonds
Of utter destruction.

(From Book XXII)

THE BED OF ODYSSEUS

     Meanwhile, the housekeeper
Eurynome bathed great-hearted Odysseus, now
In his own home again, and when she had rubbed him with oil
She helped him into a beautiful tunic and mantle.
And Athena, daughter of Zeus, shed beauty abounding
Upon him. She made him seem taller and stronger and caused
His hair to curl like the hyacinth in bloom. As a craftsman
Who learned his art from Hephaestus and Pallas Athena
Overlays silver with gold and produces a work
Full of charm, so the goddess shed grace on the head and shoulders
Of Odysseus. And he came from the bath with the form and looks
Of an immortal god and sat down again in the chair
He had left across from his wife. Then he spoke to her thus:
     "Mysterious woman! apparently those who live
On Olympus gave you a heart more hard and unyielding
Than they did to any other truly feminine woman.
Surely no other wife would be so unfeeling
As to treat standoffishly a husband who had just come back
To her and his own native land after nineteen long years
Of misery and toil. But enough! Nurse, go make up
A bed for me. I'll sleep alone, since surely
My wife has a heart of solid iron!"
     And Penelope
Shrewdly replied: "No less mysterious man!
Really I'm not at all standoffishly proud
Or scornful of you, nor is the amazement I feel
Excessive. It's just that I have such a vivid memory
Of you as you were when you boarded that long-oared ship
And said good-by to Ithaca. But go, Eurycleia,
Make the big bed for him—outside the bedroom
He himself built. Put the strong bed out there
And make it with fleeces and blankets and lovely bright spreads."

So she spoke, to see what her husband would say.
And Odysseus lost his composure and angrily spoke
To his clever and faithful wife: "Truly, woman,
Those words were bitter and painful! Who has moved
My bed? No easy job, I can tell you, no matter
How skilled a man were, though a god if he wished might come
And easily put it elsewhere. But no mere mortal
Alive, however young and lusty, would find it
Easy to pry that bed out of place—for I alone
Built it, and a greatly unusual feature went into
The careful construction of that elaborate bed.
A long-leafed olive tree grew in the court,
A fine and flourishing tree as thick as a pillar,
And I built up my bridal chamber around it with stone
On sturdy stone, thoroughly roofed it over,
And finished it up by hanging the jointed tight doors.
Then I cut off the long-leafed foliage, trimmed the trunk up
From the root, and expertly rounded it smooth and straight
With an adze. Thus I fashioned a post for the bed and bored it
All with an auger. From this beginning, I went on
With the work till I finished, richly inlaying the frame
With gold and silver and ivory and lacing it well
With thongs of crimson leather. This I describe
Was our secret, woman! But whether that bed is still solidly
There, or whether some man has cut through the stump
Of olive and moved the bed elsewhere, I wouldn't know."
        Struck by her husband's perfect description of the tokens
Between them, her heart beat fast and faster and her knees
Began to tremble. With a burst of tears, she ran straight
To Odysseus and threw her arms about his neck,
Kissing his head, and saying: "O don't be angry
With me any more, Odysseus. You were always more

Understanding than anyone else. Our misery came
From the gods, who begrudged us the joy of spending our youth
Together and coming to old age's threshold at last.
So don't be cross with me and resentful because
At first sight I didn't greet you this way. I've always
Shuddered to think that some man might come here
And take me in with his story, for those who would plot
Such evil to profit themselves are many. Surely,
Helen of Argos would never have gone to bed
With that man from abroad if she had had any notion
That the fighting sons of Achaeans would fetch her back home
To her own dear country. But a goddess made even her,
Zeus's own daughter, succumb to that miserable business,
Nor had she ever so much as imagined that she
Would be subject to that horrible infatuation—the beginning of all
Our troubles, too! But now that you have described
So well the secrets of our bed, known only to you
And me and just one other—the chambermaid Actoris,
Given to me by my father before I came here,
The one who kept the door of our strong bridal chamber—
Now my heart is convinced, hard though it is."
        Her words made him feel even more like weeping than ever,
And weep he did, with his dear and loyal wife
In his arms. And to her he was as welcome as sight
Of land to swimmers whose sturdy ship Poseidon
Has battered and shattered at sea where wind and big wave
Beat hard upon it, and sweet indeed is the moment
When the few survivors, having swum inshore and struggled
Their way through the surf, set foot at last on dry land
And escape the treacherous sea with their bodies all crusted
With brine. Such was the gladness she felt to welcome
Her husband again, as she feasted her eyes upon him
And could not for a moment take her white arms from his neck.

(From Book XXIII)

A Note on the Author

Ennis Rees was born in Newport News, Virginia, in 1925. He graduated from William and Mary and took his M.A. and Ph.D. degrees at Harvard. Before joining the faculty of the University of South Carolina, where he is a Professor of English, he taught at Duke and Princeton. His study, *The Tragedies of George Chapman: Renaissance Ethics in Action,* was published in 1954 by the Harvard University Press, and his verse translation of the *Odyssey* by Random House in 1960. This was followed by the *Iliad* in 1963. Both poems have been reprinted in the Modern Library, and among the record albums Mr. Rees has made for Spoken Arts are two of selections from his Homer. A book of his poems was published by the University of South Carolina Press in 1964, and *Fables from Aesop* by the Oxford University Press in 1966. He has written a number of books of verse especially for children, including *Riddles, Riddles Everywhere, The Song of Paul Bunyan and Tony Beaver, Tiny Tall Tales, Brer Rabbit and His Tricks, The Little Greek Alphabet Book,* and *Potato Talk.* He lives in Columbia with his wife and three children.